Over and Over the Road

Over and Over the Road, A Truck Driver's Stories

V. W. Sheperd

Copyright © 2014 V. W. Sheperd
All rights reserved.

ISBN: 149915965X
ISBN 13: 9781499159653
Library of Congress Control Number: 2014907372
CreateSpace Independent Publishing Platform
North Charleston, South Carolina

Also by V. W. Sheperd

Unbound Magnificence

Unbound Magnificence is no "little book of poetry." Consisting of nearly three hundred easy-to-read poems, this outstanding collection of modern American poetry rejuvenates you through startlingly vivid experiences of nature.

In the vein of Robert Frost, V. W. Sheperd's poems focus on the beauty of nature's ordinary moments, from simple encounters with wild animals to reflections on a rainy evening.

Sheperd paints amazing pictures with the color of words. Watch *Ducks at Whisper Marsh,* listen to *The Wind Play a Song,* spend a *Morning on the River,* and find *Where Daydreams Dwell.* All of this and more awaits you.

CONTENTS

Introduction	xi
The Ambulance	1
Pool Romance	2
New York City	2
It Must Be Hot In China	9
Driven	11
Good Morning	11
The Challenge	12
My Sense of Humor	14
The Weasel and the Rabbit	14
I Smile	16
Three Days on My Way to an Accident	17
Nuts or What?	29
Threat	32
Busy Hands	33
Tossed Blanket	33
Steve	34
They Dance	38
Someone Still Cares	39
Indomitable	40
Out of the Sky	41
You Aren't Going To Drink That Then Drive, Are You, Driver?	42
What Words Softly	43
Try Another Day	43
Like Part of the Earth It Will Soon Become	44

Moonlight Mishap	45
It Is Not So Good Anymore	49
Ouch!	52
Pumps	53
Sweet Salvation	54
Safety Glass	55
Paper Woman	56
Just As Betty Said	57
How Not to Say No	61
Slip Slide Away	62
Shaking	63
Big, Dumb, Slow Truck—Small, Smart, Fast Car	67
I Work Hard Enough Already	68
In a Second Of Seeing	69
Accidental Seduction	69
In a Flurry of Wings	70
Coveting the Beautiful	71
Howdy, Ma'am, Would You Like To Dance?	72
Smoking	73
Always To Wonder	74
Your Truck Is on Fire	75
The Show	76
Bye-Bye Baby	77
The Ball and the Brake	78
Look at These Poor Fools Driving in This Rainstorm in the Dark	79
When Birds	80
Angel	80
Crossover Consequence	83
I'm Not Supposed to Do This, She Says	85
Kirk Is a Curious Kid	88
Man Has Seen The Pictures	90
Frightened at Flagstaff	92
A Hurricane Will Soon Hit the Florida Panhandle	93
Jolly Roger	94
It Just Makes Me Wonder	97

Big And Sweet	98
Morning Star	100
She Calls Me Daddy	101
A Dark Rain	102
What Do Horses Know of Love?	104
Right Sided	104
Angry, Young Men	105
Stupid Truck Driver	106
Beyond the Wall	107
Because I'm Black	108
Something Odd Appears	110
Well, That Driver Is Probably…	110
And You	112
The Difference Between Right and Wrong	113
Do You Know What I Would Really Like to Have?	115
I Know Where Your Wheel Is	116
A Moment Of Peace	119
She Doesn't Do It on Purpose, Just Out of Ignorance	120
A Hard Time	121
The Journey Home	135
Glossary or Things You Should Know to Better Understand the Stories	139

INTRODUCTION

Over and Over the Road is a collection of short stories about my experiences and life as a forty-eight-state, over-the-road truck driver, my observations of the world around me during that time, and stories of different people I met. I drove more than a million miles over the same highways—thus the book's title. I lived in a high-rise semi (tractor trailer) for over ten years, staying on the road for up to three months at a time and taking a week or so off at the homes of friends and family in different locations in the Northwest and Arizona. By the time I started writing this book, it was impossible to achieve any chronological order or remember the where and the when. Yet what happened remained vividly etched in my mind, which is why I chose a short-story format. I drove hundreds of miles a day almost constantly, which means the circumstances repeatedly changed and were unpredictable. The book is meant to convey that, which is why, when reading the stories, you never know where you will be or what will happen next.

People say to me, "Wow, you got to travel all over the country. It must have been exciting seeing all those different places." Yet I drove mostly interstate highways and kept on a schedule. Sure, I saw the St. Louis Arch, canyons in Utah, and mountains in Oregon, but consider where sixty-five feet of truck can reasonably go. It's a challenge that never lets up. An aspiring driver said to me, "I have a friend who drives a semi, and he promised to take me out into a field and teach me how to drive." As if shifting gears is all there is to truck driving. There is so much to learn, especially the first year. After a couple of months, a driver might think he has it—piece of cake and no problem—only to roll his truck in a Wyoming snowstorm. Get cocky, and get into trouble. This job punches you in so many ways. The thirty days of truck-driving school and six weeks with a trainer are but a whiff of what a driver needs to survive out there. *Over and Over the Road* is what happened to me.

V. W. Sheperd

PS: Read the glossary at the back of the book for a better understanding of the stories. Go ahead, turn to the back of the book and have a look.

THE AMBULANCE

On a cloudy night, fast traffic rushes down the interstate highway, curving back and forth, winding along through the hills. Another truck and I overtake a slower truck in the right lane and move left to pass. I'm behind, my forward sight blocked. As we follow a curve, I glimpse flashing lights ahead and think they are on the other side of the guardrail separating the four traffic lanes, as there isn't a median. Abruptly, the truck in front of me switches back into the right lane, close in front of the slower truck. As he does, I see that immediately ahead sits an ambulance parked in the left lane.

"Shit!" I exclaim, braking hard, and the engine brake emits a loud staccato, alerting two medics behind the ambulance. Almost in unison, they dive over the guardrail. In those brief seconds, I panic. Then the two trucks beside me separate, and seeing this, I sharply swing into the right lane between them, barely missing the ambulance's open rear door as the three of us speed off into the night.

What can I say? This scared the hell out of me.

POOL ROMANCE

In the hot Arizona sun, he has on a dark blue T-shirt, and she a purple one. He sits on the edge of the motel whirlpool, and she stands on the first step, her obvious pregnancy bulging out from her small, slim form. She seems almost a child, so young. He stands taller, stronger, and a little older. Moving to the pool, she wades, and he dives into the cold April water. They come together, and he holds her as if dancing with only his feet touching the bottom. Smoothly he swirls her around in the water, and she kisses him on the cheek. They separate and move around each other, coming close many times but not touching, instead smiling, teasing, until touching in an easy, comfortable manner, she, innocent and sweet and he, her champion.

NEW YORK CITY

On my first solo trip into New York City, I apprehensively approach the George Washington Bridge from New Jersey as traffic presses tightly around my truck, jockeying for preferred toll lanes leading to the bridge. When the lanes divide for upper and lower level, allowing only a two or three-second choice, I don't know which level best suits trucks or whether it matters. I hesitate, and the traffic blocks me into the lower-level approach in the outside right lane. This doesn't concern me until

I see ahead a concrete pillar flush with the edge of the lane as the lane slightly bends right.

Damn! How can I pass that pillar without hitting it with the trailer? I should move left one lane, but I can't because the traffic hems me in. Still, I do what I can, pressing left slightly over the line. As I pass the pillar, I cannot see it. Holding my breath, I half expect to hear a loud scrape as the trailer drags against the concrete. As I slow in response to this worry, cars jam up behind, fly around, and sharply cut in front of me. Yet I breathlessly slip past the pillar unscathed and am surprised. *How did that happen?* I don't know.

Shortly, reaching the backup at the tollbooths, I confront red taillights flashing as cars and trucks brake. Then the traffic rolls forward, and I ease into the flow. For twenty minutes, sandwiched cars and trucks, and I inch forward until I am at the booth, paying the toll and passing through, gradually gaining speed and blending into the rushing traffic stream.

I reach Interstate 895, exit, and follow that highway a mile or two, carefully watching for my exit. When I see it, I blurt out, "Oh no, the ramp is closed. Now what do I do?" Yet what can I do except keep going? I reach another tollbooth and bridge, though a much smaller one than the George Washington. At the booth, I tell the attendant about the closed exit and ask him how to find my customer's address.

"I don't live around here," he says, "and I can't tell you how to get there."

"Then, please, can you tell me where to turn around?"

"You will have to cross the bridge and pay the toll, but you can turn around in the space on the other end and come back, but you will have to pay the toll that way, too."

"Are you sure I can turn around there?"

"Yeah, trucks do it all the time."

I easily complete a U-turn to come back through the booth and pay the toll. Now heading north on I-895, and knowing construction also blocks the northbound exit, I just guess and randomly pick an exit. As I come off the ramp, bewildered and afraid, I see a young black man gesturing and pointing up to suggest a low underpass, a common New York con used on truck drivers. Because I feel desperately lost, however, I hope this jive man can help me. Therefore, when he approaches, I roll down the window.

"You can't go that way, man," he says. "There's a low bridge that way. You'll get stuck. Where are you trying to go?" I give him the address and he says, "You have to turn around. Turn around, and I'll show you where it is."

"Where can I turn around?" I ask.

"Here, man, right here." He motions with his hand to the immediate street. "But let me in first. Open the door," he demands, and I do.

Turning the tractor and trailer, I almost touch the building on each side of the street. It's a tight squeeze, and I'm afraid I might get stuck, but I don't.

"Go down to the light and turn right," he tells me, pointing to a light two blocks ahead. I do that, and after a couple more blocks, he says, "At the next light, turn right."

After turning, I spot an enclosed area ahead with an entrance driveway and guard shack.

"You have to go in there, but I can't go in there, so if you'll give me sixty dollars, I will get out now."

"Sixty dollars!" I exclaim but reach for my wallet. I have seven dollars. "Here's all I've got. Now get out of my truck."

Surprisingly, he doesn't argue. He just takes the money and climbs out, slamming the door behind him. I join the procession leading to the guard shack and, after ten minutes, reach the guard.

"Who are you looking for?" the guard asks.

I give him the bills.

"That isn't in here," he says. "This is the Hunts Point Produce Market."

On hearing that, my heart sinks, but the guard continues. "Drive on through the market, staying straight, until you come to the exit. From there, turn right to the first left. They are a block and a half on the left."

"Thank you," I tell him and sigh with relief. I am, after all, not hopelessly lost. Following his directions I spot the company, but a cement divider blocks the turn. *Damn it!* Yet two blocks more and I manage to turn around. Returning, I reach the customer where, after checking in, the clerk assigns me a dock. Once at the dock, a forklift driver immediately begins unloading the trailer as I worry about where dispatch will send me to pick up and where I might park to wait for my new load. I hope this customer won't force me to leave after unloading. Before long the forklift driver finishes unloading the trailer, and I return inside for my signed bills.

"Do you have any more trucks coming in right away?" I anxiously ask the receiver. "I need somewhere to sit while I wait for a new load assignment."

"Go ahead and stay where you are. We don't have any more loads coming today," the receiver tells me.

After about an hour, I receive a message telling me to pick up a load of dirty carpet at the Jacob Javits Convention Center in Manhattan. The carpet delivers to Atlanta, Georgia, where a company will clean it for another convention. The load information doesn't include directions, so I call the convention center and an older-sounding man answers. He tells me where to exit off I-95 into Manhattan and says, "You will know it is the right exit because the ramp is covered with garbage."

Covered with garbage—is he kidding?

He continues, "Go south toward Manhattan until all the traffic is coming toward you, and you can't go any farther. You will have to turn left or right, so turn right, go a couple of blocks to Broadway, turn left," and so on.

On reaching the exit, to my amazement, garbage does indeed cover the ramp. There is not a single bare spot. As I nervously drive through the trash, I half expect to crunch glass bottles and puncture a tire, but nothing happens. From the ramp, I turn south to travel a dozen blocks until all the traffic comes toward me. I turn right to Broadway and left onto that famous avenue. At the next turn, I discover a one-way street running the wrong way. I reason that if this street runs the wrong way, the third street will also. Logically, therefore, I should take the second street, which should run the right way, and it does. But it is a narrow lane with cars parked on both sides. As I turn, I discover too late that I cannot round the corner, because the trailer will hit at least one of the cars. Yet I cannot back up into the heavy Broadway traffic either. I am stuck. I am near panic and struggle to focus. Looking around, I see pedestrians everywhere, on the sidewalks and in the street. They walk around the truck because I'm blocking the crosswalk. I am desperate enough to call out to a young man in a suit, walking with a stylishly dressed young woman, as they pass my open window.

"Excuse me, excuse me, please!" I say, projecting my voice. When he turns to me, I plead, "Could you please help me? I am stuck here. I can't back up, and I can't turn with those cars parked there." (When I think back about my plea now, I don't know what I expected him to do. I mean, it seems absurd to think he could help.)

"Uh, just a second," he says and hurries back around the truck and out of sight, leaving his companion waiting on the sidewalk.

Soon I see drivers moving their respective cars, and I am astounded. *How in the heck did he manage that? Surely the drivers weren't in their vehicles.* I don't know and cannot ask him, because afterward he comes back around, waves, and leaves with his companion. With those cars gone, I manage to complete the turn, straighten up, and pull into the narrow, congested street. The lane is barely wide enough for me to pass through, and a short distance down, the rear of a plumber's van—which was nosed into a parking space—blocks the street. As I consider this, a police officer walking by notices my predicament, and I see him calling on his radio. In about a minute, the van's driver appears and moves the van. Again I continue, until I reach a police station, where once again a parked car, a police cruiser, protrudes into the street. An officer on the sidewalk notices I have stopped. Seeing him approach the truck, I roll down the window, and he asks, "Can you get through there?"

The opening, almost exactly the width of my truck with perhaps two or three extra inches, prompts me to answer, "No way. No, sir, I cannot." I could just see myself catching onto one of those police cars. Well, in a couple of minutes, another officer appears and moves the car. Finally, I am at the end of the street with the convention center in front of me. However, I don't see a truck entrance. Being cautious, I park in a no-parking zone, hoping the police won't ticket me, and walk across the street to the convention center. There a man tells me to drive behind the center, park on the street in line with the other trucks, and wait my turn to go inside. Returning to my truck, I happily discover the police didn't ticket me. After moving my truck and parking in line with the other trucks, I quietly sit and wait my turn.

In the silence, I begin wondering why no one challenged me, why no one chewed my butt for using that street to reach the convention center when obviously a tractor trailer didn't belong there. Mulling this over, I reasoned every person in New York City undoubtedly experiences many confrontations every day. Contesting them would probably mire everyone in frustration and anger. So they learn to confront each problem with the attitude, "How can I quickly and efficiently resolve this problem and continue with my life?" I must admit, I like New Yorkers for that.

When it's my turn, a dock employee tells me to drive around to the end of the building. There a man directs me up a ramp into a narrow passage between a wall and angled docks bracketed by pillars. Trucks are everywhere, and movement is slow, deliberate, and precise. Another man points me toward a dock. With space so tightly restricted, I experience a tense fifteen minutes, yet I manage to back up to the dock without hitting any pillars or other trucks.

Before long, the loader finishes loading the carpet, and I prepare to leave. Unfortunately, at four o'clock on a Friday afternoon in Manhattan, I face horrendous rush-hour traffic. Yet, because of my hours, the legal hours I am allowed to drive, I cannot wait until the traffic thins to start. Entering the street into the heavy traffic, I discover most left turns blocked off, which prevents me from returning the way I came. Fearfully, I drive on, unsure of where I'm heading, but then I see two trucks cross on a busy street in the direction I need to go. With that left open, I turn, figuring those other trucks know the way out. But I cannot follow them because, when I am able to turn, they are gone. Still, at least now I head in the right direction and soon reach I-95. However, to my surprise and disappointment, there isn't an access ramp. Instead, to my dismay, a sign for the interstate leads me up a ramp to a maze of pillars where there isn't a light, only a stop sign. My heart drops as I realize I must cross a heavily congested, fast-moving, erratic stream of cars and trucks through the maze of pillars to reach the interstate entrance a block ahead on the other side of the street.

At the stop, a man approaches my truck waving and pointing, suggesting a low underpass. He climbs onto the driver's step and pulls himself up by grabbing the mirror supports. Bristling, I roll down the window, his face only inches from mine, and say in a stern, impatient tone, "Unless you want to go to Atlanta, get off my truck." Still he hangs on.

Ignoring him, I scan for but don't see an opening in the pell-mell, homeward-bound traffic. As I wait and watch, the traffic never breaks but charges forward as a constant, crazy, congested rush of cars. I realize I must force my way through and so tensely begin edging into the melee. As I do, my hanger-on hesitates and then drops off.

The traffic, aggressively wild, rushes by and around me, and I feel wired and afraid a car will hit me. Work-weary commuters just want me to get the hell out of their way, and I just want to get the hell out of the city. Yet, no one wants to let me through. Cars swerve around my truck, with one careening toward me, the driver honking, yelling angrily, and thrusting out his middle finger in a fit of rage while veering away in the last split second. I cannot gain any speed in the short distance to the ramp. Slowly I cut across the traffic lanes to reach the ramp, weaving around the pillars, breaking through each frenzied lane of traffic with the potential to ignite an instant pileup of dozens of cars. In sharp-edged, fearful seconds, I force my way through one…two…three lanes to finally reach the ramp, which I happily descend.

Merging onto the interstate highway, I edge snail-paced down the ramp, gradually picking up speed and blending into the traffic. As expected, this highway leads to I-95 and the George Washington Bridge, except this time I choose the upper level wide open to the sky. As I cross the bridge on my way to New Jersey and out of the city, relief rises in me, and with exhilaration I exclaim, "Thank God I am out of there."

IT MUST BE HOT IN CHINA

New York is a city of stories and, having delivered there several times, I have a few of my own. However, my first New York story occurred in my twenties, long before I became a truck driver.

In my sophomore year in college, I decided to take the summer and go to Europe. I lived in Portland, Oregon, at the time and went by train, north across Canada, east to Montreal, and south to New York City. There I spent a couple of days sightseeing before I was to board an Icelandic Airlines flight to Europe. While in New York, I had the notion of sleeping one night on a bench in Grand Central Station.

Near midnight, I sat on a bench in the station, wondering if sleeping there was okay or not. As I considered this, a woman over six feet tall with spiked heels swooped into the lobby, performing a grand entrance like a model. With long legs, long pale arms, and a narrow waist, she did the walk, the moves, for a few late-night commuters and lost souls sitting up or stretched out on the church-style wooden benches. On top of her short, coiffed hair perched a wide-brimmed hat. She was all in green—vibrant green like new leaves that first unfurl in the spring—the hat, the dress, the shoes. She strutted back and forth in front of the benches, once, twice, three times.

Finally stopping, she spoke a loud confident instruction to no one in particular. "It must be hot in China. Why don't you call Charlie and ask him?" She looked around before repeating her entreaty. "It must be hot in China. Why don't you call Charlie and ask him?"

I studied her, puzzled. No one responded, nor did it seem she expected anyone to, for after a moment's pause, she whirled away with a swish of her green dress, strode out of the station, and disappeared into the night. Watching after her for a minute or two, I half expected her to return, but she didn't. *What in the world was that about?* I wondered.

No one else seemed the least concerned. *Okay*, I thought. I stretched out and soon fell asleep. At six in the morning, an officer tapped on the bottoms of my shoes with his baton, awakening me. He told me to sit up, which I did while watching him repeat the same procedure with everyone else. Shortly, commuters filled the terminal. Gathering my belongings, I ventured outside among the crowds and was, myself, a New York story.

DRIVEN

Just after midnight, on I-10 north of Tucson, Arizona, a black car whips past and cuts in front of me to take an exit ramp at over seventy miles an hour. As I watch, it flies down the ramp, its brake lights flashing twice. Quickly reaching the end, it sharply turns right and as it does, it lifts to roll. I wonder if it's going over, but it cuts left and snaps back down. It shoots off into a grassy area to bump jump around before steering back onto the pavement and speeding away into the night.

I like this. It's a flash story, and I love to write flash stories. When I was in high school, my senior English teacher required every student to have a steno pad and write one page in it every day. I decided to try and make each page a complete story, and I wish I still had that pad. It wasn't the steno pad or what was written in it that was important, but the idea that a complete story could be written in a few lines. That appealed to me—the conciseness without all the fluff. It makes me think of haiku, Japanese poetry, and how it expresses an idea in a few words.

GOOD MORNING

Near Olive Branch, Mississippi, on an early August morning full of clear summer light, a robin stands in a shallow puddle, a narrow slip of water, alongside the road. The water reaches several inches up on her body, and she dips her head down into it, fluttering and throwing water up, on, and around her. She does this a half dozen times, pausing briefly between each dip until, obviously satisfied, she hops onto the dry pavement and flutters one last time before flying off across the road.

Now the glistening water, only slightly disturbed by a gentle breeze, reflects two trees edging the road. From the closest tree, a blackbird drops onto the mowed grass and walks with bobbing steps before stopping on the cement curb beside the water. An approaching pickup frightens him, and he abruptly flies off as the pickup passes, and it too is gone.

Afterward, the robin returns, gliding in to land on the pavement. Cautiously glancing around before hopping into the water, she dips and flutters just once before hopping out and abruptly flying away, the last cool rinse in the shower before she dresses and goes on with her day.

THE CHALLENGE

Pulling in front of a customer's warehouse, I stop and set the brake while scanning the area around the dock. What I see worries me: a single dock boxed in by a wall and a Dumpster facing the narrow street. Across from it, two large rocks sit on the edge of a manicured lawn fronting another business. Undoubtedly, drivers backing up sometimes swing onto the lawn, causing ruts and ruining the landscaping, hence the rocks. With just one week of driving solo, my backing isn't worth a damn, and I wonder how I can possibly get into that dock. The "first days on the job" worries plague me—an uneasy feeling of never being sure what the hell is happening and repeatedly asking myself, *Now what do I do?* While considering my choices, two other trucks arrive and park on the street waiting to deliver, but first here, first in, and that means me.

But I can't see how to do this. An experienced driver, by observation, knows how to position the truck to successfully back up. I cannot because I am not experienced. Therefore, I try pulling up and backing up, and when one way doesn't work, I try again from another angle. I even run the truck's nose over the curb and the lawn and nudge the rocks, but nothing works. After a while, the strain and ache in my body prompts me to wonder how many times I have attempted this. Finally, stopping to ponder what to do, I freeze in my ignorance, waiting, I suppose, for a miraculous revelation, waiting and trying to figure out what I cannot figure out. Meanwhile, the next driver in line, a woman in her thirties, approaches, and I roll down the window to receive her.

"Hi, looks like you're having some trouble. It's a tough one. I was wondering…I mean, I could put it in there for you. Would you want me to do that?"

Hell, what's a man to do? He can't let a woman help him. I hesitate, studying her and noting her manner, a stance of "I am willing to help if you will let me. I'm not trying to embarrass you."

Realizing this, I respond, "Please, that would be great." I slip out of, and she slips into, the seat and in one pull-up and backup, the trailer is in the dock.

What can I say? Backing up a sixty-five-foot tractor trailer is difficult, and it can take a long time to learn, because conditions are somewhat different every time. Hey, I'm making excuses for myself. That's all right. If that young woman hadn't helped me, I might still be there trying to do that. Ha!

MY SENSE OF HUMOR

In the early morning, at a McDonald's fast-food restaurant, I step in line behind a young man wearing a T-shirt that reads, "I ran out of sick days, so I called in dead."
 I like it.

THE WEASEL AND THE RABBIT

Having just washed my truck at the Blue Beacon truck wash at Eloy, Arizona, two attendants now hand dry the fiberglass body. When they finish, I tip five dollars to the nearer attendant and suppose he will share the money with his partner. Pulling my truck up a hundred feet, I stop and climb out to check over the job. As I look for any missed spots, an older woman, perhaps in her sixties, smartly dressed in tan slacks and a beige blouse, a curvy five foot six with dyed blond hair, approaches me.
 "Hi," she says. "I am trying to get to California. My classic has a flat on the steering, and the other one looks like it's about to blow. I need some money to buy two new tires."
 Say "classic" to a truck driver, and he or she will probably think as I did, a Freightliner Classic, a tractor trailer.
 "Won't your company buy the tires for you?"
 "My company?"
 "Yes, the company you drive for."

"The company I drive for?" she says, obviously perplexed.

"Aren't you a truck driver?"

"No, no, my classic has bad tires, and I need to get some new ones."

"Your classic is a car."

"Yes," she states, "a '66 Ford Mustang. I need about $200 for the tires and my motel room."

"You are asking for a lot," I say. "I wouldn't think two tires would cost that much."

"Well, I have to buy special tires for that car. It wouldn't do to put just any tires on it, because it is a classic. I am looking for a good Christian man to help me," she says.

"Why a Christian?" I ask.

"Well, Christians are generally more honest, more trustworthy."

"Just because someone is a Christian doesn't mean they are honest and trustworthy," I counter.

"Yes, but they usually are. You seem like a nice man. Could you lend me the money? Or better yet, if you have a credit card, we could put it on that, so I wouldn't take all of your cash. Do you have a credit card? I will send you the money after I get to California."

"No, I don't want to use my credit card. Wait here a second," I say and climb back into my truck for the cash. You may well be thinking, *Are you stupid or what?* Well, she is an older woman, attractive, stranded, and at risk. Horrible things could happen to her. I can spare the cash, and so I will trust her. Shortly, I am back on the ground and handing her the money.

"Are you sure you want to do this? I hate to take all of your cash. Wouldn't it be better to put it on your credit card?" she again asks.

"No, I would rather do it this way," I say. When she kept insisting on the credit card, I probably should have figured it was a scam. Still, maybe it wasn't.

"Well, let me give you a hug," she offers and does, pressing herself firmly against me. Afterward she steps back but stays close, looking at the truck. "Is your wife with you?"

"No, I'm not married," I say.

"I'm looking for someone," she starts. "I was going out with this Hawaiian man, but it didn't work out. I have never been with a different race before, and it was strange. I'm looking for a good Christian man. You are very nice. Can I give you another hug?" she asks.

"Yes, that's okay," I tell her, and she does. She tries to kiss me on the mouth, but I turn my cheek, and she kisses me there instead, lingering before releasing me, though still standing close.

"Can I have your address so I can return the money?" she says.

I give her the address.

"Can I have your phone number, too?"

"No, you don't need my phone number. Just send the money to that address, and that will be fine," I say.

She folds the paper, puts it into her purse, and says, "Thank you." Then she turns and walks away.

Surprise! I never got the money. This story is somewhat embarrassing. Yet I believe every man has the right to be a fool. Was I a fool? I think I probably was. I think men are often fools with women.

I SMILE

As I run I-70 in Missouri, heading to Reno, Nevada, the fast traffic pushes over the seventy-mile-an-hour speed limit. Cars and trucks pass me, some speeding eighty or more, and I think *Eighty is too fast for this road*. Rough, uneven pavement curves and rolls up and down through the hills, and these conditions dictate no one should drive over fifty-five. Yet it's a fever-pitched race and to me a little crazy; something drivers are easily caught up in. Even I feel pressured, but no, I'm not doing that. I'll stop for a while and let the traffic thin out.

Ahead I spot a Pilot truck stop with a Wendy's restaurant. I decide to stop there and buy a hamburger and a Frosty, Wendy's malted ice cream in a cup. Exiting the highway up a ramp, I turn right and right again into the Pilot's lot. I park and walk to the restaurant at the front of the lot.

At eleven o'clock, the noon rush hasn't started yet. When I approach the front counter, I am the only customer, and an older woman pleasantly and efficiently greets me. She waits patiently while I ponder what I want, because now that I study the menu board, choices other than a hamburger tempt me. Finally, I change my mind and order a taco salad. Afterward, I step back and watch her take a salad out of a cooler and ladle chili onto crisp green lettuce, my taco salad.

To her left, another clerk, a tall, young man with dark hair and his back to me, turns around. He holds a large, flat-folded, brown paper sack in front of him, his hands on the sides. I wonder what he's doing. Then, seeing written on the sack, "Will work for food," I can't help myself and smile.

THREE DAYS ON MY WAY TO AN ACCIDENT

On Sunday evening, I approach Dyersburg, Tennessee, with a load of ground limestone. I hope my receiver has parking, because my appointment isn't until one o'clock Monday afternoon. Checking the directions, I read, "Follow BR 51 north to the first light, Cedar Street, and turn left to the first stop sign. Turn left again to the customer on the left-hand side." As I follow 51 into Dyersburg, the highway divides, yet nothing says "BR." They both just say Highway 51, and I don't know what to do. I stay straight to the first light but don't see a street sign. Is this Cedar? I look everywhere for a sign—overhead, left, and right, and on every corner—but no sign. What should I do?

I decide to chance it and turn. Two blocks down the street, I pass a plant with a police officer parked in its lot, watching the traffic. After a mile I leave the city limits. The street becomes a two-lane country road, no stop sign, no left turn, no customer, just trouble, for obviously I am not on Cedar Street. Large farms surround Dyersburg, and I could drive thirty miles before I find a turnaround. In addition, night is fast approaching, and that causes me to worry still more. Who knows what hell I might meet trying to turn around in the dark?

Desperate, I scan ahead and see a possibility. There is a building with a narrow gravel yard adjoining the street and, opposite it, a service station also with a similar strip. Using both spaces and the street, I believe I can complete the turn. With the road clear in both directions, I pull into the shallow gravel lot, swinging as wide right as possible. Turning left, I cross the street to the gas pumps. Cutting close to the service station overhang, I loop through the turn smoothly and efficiently and pull the truck around. Because I block both lanes, I worry a car I cannot see coming down the road might slam into my truck. Yet, soon I am safely around and headed back into town.

Near the yard where I saw the officer, I watch my speed, because the limit slows to twenty-five miles an hour. I guess the officer waits to catch drivers not slowing down as they come into town. He is still there, and I slowly drive by in the dark, the night now having overtaken me. Retracing my route, I turn south on Highway 51, looking for BR 51, but unfortunately, I miss the cutoff in the dark. Spotting a large gravel pullout, I make a U-turn and head back north on 51. Coming to the split again, this time I take the right fork. After about two miles, I come to the first light, and again no street sign. I look everywhere but see no sign. *What's wrong with this town?* I turn left and hope this time I am right. Watching, I finally see one reading, "Cedar Street." Thank God. After three or four blocks, I come to a stop and, turning left, see the customer. I am relieved that I finally made it.

At the guard shack, the guard asks, "Can I help you?"

"My appointment isn't until tomorrow, and I was hoping you have somewhere for me to park."

"You can park in the gravel lot across the street," he tells me.

"Okay, thank you." Pulling back into the street and stopping in front of the lot, I realize I have to blindside back around a telephone pole in the dark. There is no way I am doing that! Blindside backing in the dark around a telephone pole sucks. Therefore, I continue down the street and look for a turnaround. After a couple of blocks, I see another officer parked and watching the street and, just past him, a sign reading, No Trucks. Damn!

The officer pulls behind me but doesn't turn on his lights, perhaps because there isn't anywhere to pull off, and stopping me would mean blocking the street. Apprehensively, I keep going until I see a stop sign ahead. I decide to take the initiative before he does. Stopping, I turn on my four-ways, exit the truck, and walk back to the police car. The officer rolls down his window.

"Hi! I am supposed to deliver to PolyOne, but my appointment isn't until tomorrow. PolyOne said park in their lot, but I couldn't, and I couldn't turn around. I don't know how to get out of here or where to park. Could you help me, please?"

He scowls and sternly responds, "You are not on the truck route."

"Well, when I couldn't get in their lot, there wasn't anything I could do but keep going. I hoped there was somewhere to turn around, but there isn't," I tell him.

"Why don't you park in their other lot?" he asks.

"I didn't know they have another lot," I reply.

"Yes, they do," and he gives me directions. Apparently realizing I have no idea what he's talking about, he says with disgust, "Just follow me; I'll take you there."

I follow him, and he takes me to a lot a block from PolyOne. As I park in a slot between two trailers, he leaves. Looking around, I am bothered because there is a different name on the building and trailers, not PolyOne. Damn! Well, I hope no one will bother me, because I cannot do any more. I am tired and need to sleep. I sleep through the night undisturbed and, in the morning, walk to PolyOne. A different guard tells me I parked at a division of their company, and I need to move to the lot across the street.

"I don't think I can get in there," I say.

"You don't have to pull into a space, just park in front of the trailers," he says.

This I do but don't like it, because two other trucks managed to properly park, and I'm now blocking them. Another truck tries parking but cannot and continues down the street. When he returns, I am surprised and wonder how he managed to turn around when I couldn't. He easily backs into a space. There are still two spaces left, and I decide I should also drive down the street, turn around, come back, and properly park. I reason that if he turned around, I can, too. However, heading down the street and carefully looking for possibilities, I don't see anywhere he could have turned. I again reach the No Trucks sign and, of course, have to keep going. Fortunately, the officer isn't there.

After another five blocks, I reach the main road where I turn north until I spot a large shopping center where I turn around and head back south. But I still need to park in that lot, and I only see one sensible choice: return up Cedar through the no-trucks zone and hope the officer doesn't catch me. Talk about pushing your luck—and in a town with officers everywhere. Yet,

I do just that, practically holding my breath all the way. Now at the lot, facing the right direction, I easily park.

As I wait, another truck tries to make a U-turn around the telephone pole, and I watch him, thinking, there is no way you can do that, buddy. As he turns, his trailer bumps against the pole, and he stops. He cannot see the pole and perhaps thinks he has just hit a curb, a rock, or a rough spot or whatever. He doesn't get out and look. He backs up slightly and tries again, but this time pushes hard. When he does, the top of the pole jerks back and forth, causing the wires to jump. "Damn!" I loudly exclaim. I wonder if he can snap the pole off at the ground. If that pole comes down, there will be one hell of a mess. I should stop him. Yet I don't want to be outside with those hot wires if that pole does come down. Finally, he stops but still doesn't get out and look. Instead he backs up again, and I think, *Oh God, here we go.* Yet, he keeps backing up until he is again in the street where he turns and drives away toward the No Trucks sign. I watch for him to return, but he doesn't, and I wonder if the officer got him.

Shortly, the guard heads my way, for I don't have a CB. He directs me to a warehouse and tells me to back into any open dock. I do that, and after fifteen minutes (it has been sixteen hours since I first arrived), they have me unloaded. Once I have my paperwork, I leave the plant looking for a parking space to wait for my next load. I spot a vacant warehouse with an unfenced lot where I probably couldn't park overnight, but for a few hours, I doubt anyone will care.

Dispatch could take several hours to assign me a load, and meanwhile I have something else to deal with. The shipper didn't seal the powdered limestone containers, and they leaked because of the constantly vibrating trailer. Now a white dust coats the trailer floor. The load instructions require I wash out the trailer after unloading; however, Dyersburg doesn't have any truck washes. I hope my next load isn't a food product, because that shipper probably wouldn't load this trailer. Yet, if I wash the trailer, they may not load a wet trailer either. So I sweep it out but cannot sweep out all the white dust. When I finish, the floor doesn't look much better than when I started. However, perhaps I will get lucky, and the next customer won't care about limestone dust.

At 3:00 p.m., the Qualcomm beeps, and I receive a new load without a pickup number that picks up at Frito-Lay at Jonesboro, Arkansas. Pass the potato chips with the ground limestone, please. How the limestone would get into the potato chip bags, I cannot guess. Yet, for sure, Frito-Lay will not load this trailer when they see white dust on the floor. For the next three hours, I repeatedly ask dispatch where to wash the trailer and for a load number but to no avail. Finally, dispatch tells me to sweep out the trailer and not to worry about the load number, but if I have any problems at Frito-Lay to let them know. They give me the "shoo, shoo, go away and stop bothering us" routine, because by the time I reach Jonesboro, they will have gone home.

I know I will need a load number to pick up the load and that Frito-Lay won't load this dusty trailer. However, the closest truck wash is at West Memphis, Arkansas, fifty miles out of route. That won't work, but I have a brilliant idea. Ha!

I carry two gallons of water in case of a water leak, because when the truck has a leak, and the water level in the radiator falls below a certain point, the truck's computer automatically shuts down the engine. Because of this, I carry extra water to enable me to drive the truck to a shop or truck stop. I decide to pour the water onto the floor of the trailer and, using the broom, blend and smear the white dust in with the darker trailer dust. My plan is to change the eye-striking white to the usual dark floorboard. The plan works, somewhat, though at first the wet floor disguises the result.

However, in the sweltering heat (inside the trailer is a cooker, and I am drenched with sweat), the floor rapidly dries. When it does, I have a smeary-looking floor that's still white, but not bone white and, though better, perhaps not good enough.

Well, it's the best I can do. I will just have to go and see what happens. Jonesboro, Arkansas, lies a hundred miles, or about two hours away, and I arrive at Frito-Lay about ten thirty at night. Entering the building, I find a phone with instructions for calling the receiving office, which I do.

"Hello," a woman answers.

"Hello, I am a driver picking up a load headed to Laredo, Texas, but I don't have a load number." I believe I know what she will say, and she does.

"I cannot help you without a load number," she responds. "You will have to call your dispatcher."

What can I say except okay and hang up? Back in the truck, I send a Qualcomm message, "Need a pickup number." Promptly, I receive the reply, "Working on it." Well, a half-dozen hours and messages later, they are still working on it. Finally, they tell me, "Check back tomorrow after 7:00 a.m. central time, no pickup number yet," and so I go to bed. At 6:00 a.m., a knock on my door awakens me. When I move aside the blackout curtain, I discover a man looking up at me. He wears our company cap, so he is one of our drivers. Rolling down the window, I ask him what he wants.

"I don't have a load number," he tells me. "I spoke with a woman in the shipping department, and she said our company doesn't have any loads until Thursday."

I have only had three hours sleep and so groggily ask him, "What day is this?"

"Tuesday," he answers. After we exchange several irrelevant remarks, he returns to his truck.

Still feeling sleepy and tired, I go back to bed. When I awake at 9:30 a.m., there still isn't a message, and I shoot one off about what the other driver told me.

Shortly, a message comes back. "You are off load."

Hooray! Now perhaps dispatch will assign me a shipper unconcerned about loading this trailer. After a while, I receive a message to drive to our drop yard in Memphis, Tennessee, where another driver will split a load that dispatch has assigned to me. That means I can drop this trailer, hooray! When I reach our Memphis yard where I drop my limestone trailer, I check around and discover my load isn't there yet. After a while, I receive a message telling me the load has finally arrived. Walking the yard, I spot the trailer, but a truck sits parked in front of it.

Four people stand beside the truck, an older couple and two young men, and there is a problem. The driver's side aluminum step flares up and away, and I hear one young man explaining why. He went inside a truck stop, and when he came back, the step was like that, implying another truck was responsible. The older man thinks he can bend the step back well enough so the damage will be hardly noticeable. However, to do this he needs tools. I hear him asking the driver if he has any, but the driver doesn't, and so he asks me.

"Yes, I have tools," I tell him, which I supply.

The older man tries different tools to bend the step: a crowbar, a hammer, a load strap, a load bar, and various wrenches, screwdrivers, and pliers, gradually managing to get the step almost back to normal. Now I need to leave, having waited while they worked on the step.

"I am assigned this trailer. Please pull away from it, so I can hook up," I tell the driver.

"I can't. My truck won't start."

"Huh? Okay. Did you call breakdown? Are they sending help?"

"They just said to check the water and oil," he answers.

"So did you check them?" I ask, annoyed.

"I think they are all right," he says.

"So did you call breakdown back and tell them?" I persist.

"No, I didn't," he says.

By now I am tense and irritated. Then the old man interrupts.

"You're supposed to take that load?" he asks.

"Yes," I reply.

"Well, we can move the tractor. He's unhooked from the trailer, so towing him off with your tractor should be a simple matter," he tells me.

I think that will probably work. I back up to the disabled truck, and the older driver hooks up a fiberglass load strap between us. When I start out, the strap breaks. Climbing out of the cab I say, "Oh, you know what? I have a tow chain, which I use so seldomly I forgot I have it." The tow chain doesn't break, and soon we have the disabled tractor moved.

By now, night has fallen, and I am eager to start out. Quickly hooking up, I leave the drop yard at 9:30 p.m. I head east on I-240, the loop around Memphis, unaware of what is about to happen. As the loop turns north, I travel in the middle lane of three lanes with no one around me, even though I can see in my mirror the lights of three or four cars about one mile back. I decide this would be a good time to move into the right lane before the traffic catches me. Looking right, I don't see anything, so I signal and begin moving right.

Bang, I hit something. A few seconds later, *boom*. The trailer sharply fishtails two or three times. "What the hell," I blurt out, startled. Easing back into the center lane, I steady the wheel until the truck again acts normally. My mind races to discover what happened. I saw nothing in the right lane and, as I again look, I still don't. However, I know I hit something. I thought I had a blowout, but now the truck handles all right, and this confuses me. I don't know what happened, but I know I'm in trouble. Scanning my mirrors, I see a ways behind me the lights of a car dropping back. It drives onto the shoulder and stops. *That must be the one*, I think. Yet why couldn't I see it before?

As I move onto the shoulder, the other traffic overtakes me and swiftly passes. Using the Qualcomm, I notify my fleet manager of the accident. Afterward, I get out and run the distance back to check on the other driver. As I approach the car, someone rolls down the window, and I see a woman alone in the car.

"Are you okay?" I inquire.

"Uh, yes, I believe so," she replies.

"I will back my truck up closer to your car," I tell her.

"Okay," she says, and I hurry back to my truck.

Checking the tractor and trailer for damage, I only find a scratched aluminum passenger's side drive wheel with the plastic lug nut caps missing. That accounts for the shimmying motion of the trailer, which occurred when the trailer ran over the caps. Checking my tires, I don't find a blowout, which had to be the boom, so the blowout must have been on her car. Climbing into the cab, I slowly back up with my four-ways on and stop twenty-five feet from her car. Once stopped, I use my cell phone to call our safety hotline, and the supervisor questions me.

"Were the police called?"

"No," I respond. "Do we have to call the police on an accident like this?" I know if someone calls the police, I will probably receive a ticket that will become part of my record and possibly have serious consequences for me.

"No, but if she wants to call them, she has the right to do so," he tells me.

"Okay," I reply and hang up.

Taking my phone, I climb from the truck and, removing the reflector triangles from my side compartment, arrange them to the rear of her car. When I inspect the car, a four-door Pontiac Grand Prix, I see my wheel scraped and dented the rear passenger door and the panel over the rear wheel on the driver's side. The black plastic wraparound bumper shows a slight scrape also, and the rear tire is flat. As I finish inspecting the car, the driver emerges. I say to her, "We need to exchange information." Afterward I hand her the phone saying, "You can use this to call anyone you need to."

"I want to call the police," she says. I am unhappy with that but leave it alone.

"Do you have a spare?" I ask her.

"Yes, I do," she responds. She opens the trunk, uncovers the spare, removes the jack, and hands it to me.

I change the tire while she sits in her car calling, I presume, the police. Soon she gets out and returns my phone, telling me what she has learned.

"The police won't be able to come right away, but they should be here in a while," she tells me. Then she stands quietly, watching me change the tire.

After a moment I wonder if she called her family or anyone who might be awaiting her arrival, so I ask, "Did you call your family so they won't worry?"

"Yes, I did," she replies, appearing surprised. After a long pause, she says, "Thank you."

"You're welcome," I answer and continue with the tire.

As I close the trunk after finishing with the tire, a police officer arrives, pulling up to the triangles, his red lights circling and flashing, his headlights blinking. As he does, my apprehension ratchets up a notch. He climbs from his car and, as he approaches, I see he is a small young man.

"I'm sorry it took so long," he apologizes. "I was on another call. I will talk to the other driver first."

"Okay," I say and hang around his car, waiting. When he returns, we sit in the patrol car, and he asks me what happened. I tell him.

"You wouldn't have had to call the police, you know," he says sympathetically. "My dad was a driver, so I know how problems can build up on a driver's record. I am sorry we had to meet this way."

"Well, she wanted to call, and she has the right to do so. I know that isn't best for me, but that's the way it is," I say. I'm thinking the officer is likable, but his remark about "meeting this way" seems odd to me, because we haven't met in the true sense. He is a police officer, and he is going to give me a ticket.

"I have to give you a ticket," he says apologetically.

"Yes, I know." As he completes the paperwork, the rain starts, lightly and almost unnoticed. After he finishes, he hands me the ticket and tells me how to comply with it. I take the ticket and say, "I will have her move her car a few feet so I can be sure the wheel works correctly."

"Okay," he says, and as he does, heavier rain splatters on the windshield.

Tucking the ticket into my pocket, I open the door. As I step out of the car, the sky dumps a torrent of water. "Shit," I exclaim loudly. The rain drenches me, soaking my shirt, pants, shorts, socks, and shoes almost instantly. The sudden reality of being sopping wet stops me for a moment, but then I walk around the rear of the Pontiac through the deluge and tap on the driver's window. She doesn't roll down the window, so I tell her through the glass to move her car so I can check that the wheel works, When she drives a short way, the wheel turns normally, not wobbling. So I tell her she can leave, and she does.

After picking up my safety triangles, I replace them in the side box of my cab as the soaking downpour continues. The rain floods the highway with a rolling sheet of water. Once inside my truck, I change my clothes, occasionally looking in my mirrors to see if the officer is still there, and he is. Unless he gets a call, he will probably stay there, protecting me with his lights until I leave. Soon, on completing my logs, I signal and pull out onto the highway into the flow of traffic. After a couple of miles, I exit to I-40 east, rolling on toward Nashville, worrying in the long empty hours whether my employer will fire me.

Everything in this story happened as I wrote it. I suppose the story is a bit tedious, yet somehow seems important, because truck driving—for me, at least—wasn't just a job. It was how I lived day-to-day, and this is an example not just for me but for truck driving in general, or at least so I think.

NUTS OR WHAT?

On a pleasantly warm Easter Sunday, I sit parked at our Phoenix, Arizona, terminal and, after a while, decide to go inside. Leaving the truck and walking the short distance to the main building, I enter the drivers' lounge. Inside a commercial plays on the television. A dogsled, with the driver wrapped in a thick, fur-fringed, hooded jacket, pushes across the ice-and-snow-covered tundra. Behind it a second sled appears with men positioned as dogs. They run on all fours pulling the sled with wild exertion, mimicking the motion of the dogs while a dog rides, guiding the sled. Huh? I laugh. What a hilarious absurdity. I have no idea what this is about. Yet this craziness fits the last couple of days, like the group whipping an Easter rabbit in an Easter presentation. Supposedly they intended to give the children a more direct connection to the crucifixion of Christ.

Then, yesterday, at the Ehrenberg, Arizona, Flying J, as I walked toward the store, a Kenworth tractor trailer sped into the truck stop too fast for a parking lot. As I neared the fuel islands, he looped around and headed back and straight toward me. I felt threatened and was tempted to bolt and run. Still, I restrained myself as he bore down on me, stopping hard five feet from me, dangerously close. Angrily, I glared up at him, but I couldn't see him through the reflected light from the windshield. As I went inside, he pulled through where I had stood and backed into a parking space. Finishing in the store, I came out, and as I did, the Kenworth driver exited his truck and walked toward me.

Smiling, he said, "Hi, how are you doing?"
"You know, you could have hit me," I said to him.
"I scared you, huh?" he said, smiling, obviously pleased.
"Your foot could have slipped off the brake pedal."
"No, I wouldn't do that."

I wanted to smash his ridiculous smiling face. Afterward I wanted to bust out his headlights, a bad idea. Later, I thought I should have switched the two air lines connected to the trailer, a harmless prank. He wouldn't be able to move his truck until he discovered the crossed lines. That would have pleased me, except by then I was halfway to Phoenix. Yet this wasn't the end of the craziness.

When I reached Phoenix, the interstate expanded to five lanes with moderately heavy and fast traffic. As I kept the pace, two cars, one from each lane on either side of me, simultaneously swung in front of me. As they did, the car farthest in front made a jerking motion. Did they collide? I don't know. I didn't see if they did, but they hit their brakes, abruptly slowing and stopping unexpectedly in front of me. "Damn," I exclaimed. I quickly scanned the adjacent lanes, but several cars blocked them, leaving nowhere for me to go. I jammed the brake hard—yet controlled and steady—to avoid a jackknife. Instantly, black smoke emitted from my tires as I laid black lines on the pavement, but I didn't stop, not yet, maybe never. In the brief seconds, I worried *I might not stop in time.* "Stop, stop," I told my truck. Four feet from the rear car, the truck finally stopped. Whew!

A huffy, thickset woman pushed from the front car as a man appeared from the car nearest me. Their attitudes said he clipped her, but I couldn't see any damage. If there was any, it couldn't have been much. Yet they stood in the center of the seventy-mile-an-hour freeway fussing about a scratch. How stupid were they? Well, they pulled in front of an eighty-thousand-pound behemoth and stopped. They could be dead. But they didn't even notice me a few feet behind them. They didn't get it, didn't see it at all. I thought, *I have to leave and fast. Any second another truck or car might rear-end my truck or smash into him and her.*

From their behavior, I believe they thought, *Hey, we had our little accident now, so give us our space. You cannot hit us. It isn't allowed.* Wow, is that ever stupid. These two nitwits quibbled over a scratch with their lives in immediate danger. Watching for an opening, I moved right with my flashers on, hoping the other traffic saw me and recognized I barely moved. Gradually, I picked up speed and finally reached a safe range again. A couple of miles farther down the road I intended to exit and fuel at the Flying J Truck Stop, but because I wasn't sure which exit it was, I missed the exit. *No problem, I will drive to the next exit, about a mile farther, and turn around.*

Reaching the exit, I started up the ramp, only to see a tractor trailer, a pickup, and a car in front of me behaving oddly. They swerved around one another, the car even driving onto the banked concrete shoulder. Seeing this, I slowed and stopped a ways behind them as they reached the red light at the end of the ramp. *What in the world is happening?* As I watched, the car turned right around the corner and disappeared. The pickup waited in the left lane, and the tractor trailer in the right lane. I saw both drivers yelling and gesturing at each other. They emerged from their vehicles, and I wondered if they would fight. Facing off, they yelled and shook their fists. I watched for a blow. Yet after a couple of minutes of blustering, they returned to their respective trucks, still yelling and gesturing. When the light changed, they drove on, one left and one right, and I thought, *Wow, is everyone in Phoenix nuts or what?*

THREAT

On hearing a knock, I open the Phoenix motel room door to a Hispanic woman with a housekeeping cart. "Do you need service today?" she asks.

"Yes, you can come in," I tell her. Yet she doesn't enter.

"I cannot clean the room with you in it, sir, and the manager is right over there," she says, nodding her head toward an older man and a middle-aged woman conversing on the other side of the pool.

"Oh, okay. I can sit out by the pool until you finish," I say. Gathering my laptop, I retreat outside. She enters the room and pulls the wide cart across the opening, blocking access. After a couple of minutes, I see her push the cart sideways to get the vacuum cleaner from the end of the cart. Afterward, she again pulls the cart across the doorway. This suggests to me that guests or strangers have likely attacked housekeepers in the past. Now the management considers everyone a possible threat. But I believe losing her job for disobeying the rules concerns her more than someone attacking her.

Shortly, she finishes and smiles at me as she pushes her cart to the next room, again knocking. This time no one answers. "Housekeeping," she says loudly. She knocks again and, after no response, repeats, "Housekeeping." With no response again, she opens the door with her pass and peers cautiously around before entering. Once inside, she positions the cart, blocking the doorway, and disappears into the room.

BUSY HANDS

Waiting for the Phoenix, Arizona, terminal to repair my truck, I sit in the laundry and work on my stories. The laundry has a plug-in for my laptop. As I work, I drink grapefruit juice and soon need to use the restroom. Exiting into the hall, I walk the short way to MEN, push open the door, and step inside. What I see stops me. A young man stands at the urinal with his back to me, his left hand taking care of business while his right hand holds a pint of milk, which he chugs. Surprised, I think, *Oh my God!*

TOSSED BLANKET

Parked at our Phoenix, Arizona, terminal, I run my truck to operate the air conditioner, which, it seems, I am constantly repairing. Coincidentally, it breaks down in the sweltering summer heat when I badly need it. Lately it has worked all right. Yet, now the temperature inside my truck builds, and I begin to feel stressed. Extending my hand to a vent, I check the air, and it is cold. Why then do I feel hot and getting hotter?

As I complete my paperwork, I stop every few minutes to check the temperature, and each time cold air blows against my palm. Finally I decide to take my completed trip envelope inside to the drop box. As I exit the truck, the heat hits me like a tossed blanket, the intensity surprising me, and I briskly walk to the office. On opening the door, a cool gush of refrigerated air engulfs me, a slight shock, though refreshing.

Another driver about to go outside passes beside me, and I make an offhand remark to him. "Boy, it sure is hot today."

"Yeah, 118 degrees," he says.

STEVE

While waiting in my truck at the Traveler's Inn motel in Phoenix, Arizona, for the 2:00 p.m. check-in, I gaze through the windshield, half-lost in a daydream. I see a man come around a corner of the motel and head toward the parking lot. He has that dirty, homeless look about him. He appears young, in his late twenties, with dishwater-blond, shoulder-length hair, black T-shirt and pants, and no shoes, and he carries a shoulder bag. When I see him turn toward my truck, I realize he has spotted me and is about to hit on me, probably for money. As he approaches, I roll down the window.

"Can I do anything for you, like do you need your wheels polished or anything?" he says up at me.

"Do you have any polish?" I ask, suspecting he doesn't.

"No, I don't."

"That's okay, I have polish. How much do you want to do my two front wheels?"

"How much will you give me?" he says.

He bets his "sympathy card," supposing that because he is dirty, shoeless, and homeless, I will be generous, and he gives me the opportunity to be as generous as I want.

"Five dollars a wheel," I tell him, "and I supply the polish."

"How about if I do all the chrome for twenty?" he offers.

All the chrome includes the two front wheels, the struts on a half-dozen mirrors, and the chrome handlebars for climbing around outside the cab and for entering and exiting. Twenty dollars is a steep price for this, but he judged me correctly.

"Okay, let me find the polish for you," I say, lifting from my seat to the back of the cab. Finding polish and rags under the bed, I take them outside and hand them to him.

"I'm Steve," he says, offering his hand. "My handle is 'Static.'"

"Vernon," I respond, shaking his hand.

"Your wheels are really pitted," he says, as he starts to polish the first one. "With a high-speed buffer, I could do these real good," he says to me, which suggests he wants to put out the least possible effort, and, of course, he doesn't have a buffer.

"Yes, I know they are. Just do the best you can. They will be shiny anyhow. I'm going to Carl's Junior for a vanilla shake. Would you like one?"

"Yeah, okay," he says, before veering off on a tangent. "Did you get any of those muffins in the motel?" he asks. "They're real good. They have blueberry and banana-nut and some others. I got me three or four of them."

"I haven't checked in yet," I tell him, thinking he hasn't checked in either and never will. I figure this is just one of the ways he survives on the street. "I will return in ten minutes," I say and leave for the milk shakes.

"Yeah, okay," he answers without looking up, intent on his polishing. Ten minutes later, I return with the shakes and hand one to him.

"Thanks," he says, breaking from his work to set the shake down beside him. This is just as well, for Carl's gives you drinking straws for the milk shakes. You can bust a gut trying to suck that ice cream through the tiny hole until the ice cream starts to melt.

"It's hard living on the streets," I say to him.

"Yeah, it's hard easy," he responds with a sly smile. "There are no bills, no job to go to, and, best of all, no women ragging you."

"You had a place somewhere then?"

"Yeah, I had the whole shebang: a double-wide on five acres, a job, bills, and an old lady."

"Where was that?"

"Easley, South Carolina, between Anderson and Greenville."

"Do you have any kids?"

"No. I was raising three of hers."

"Married?"

"No, just living together."

"For how long?"

"Eight years."

"So what happened with that?"

"She was always having these jealous fits over other women."

I look at him and see a still-attractive man, sinewy, with gray-green eyes. "Did you go out with other women?"

"No, I was loyal, but she was always having these fits, and she would call the cops and get me arrested. Finally, the judge gave me a year in the county pen. He told me that when I got out, if I was ever in his courtroom again, I would get ten years in the federal pen. When the year was over, she wanted me back, and I told her if she started the jealousy thing again, I was gone. After a few months, she did, and I left. There is no way I was going to do ten years in the fed."

"How long ago was that?" I ask.

"Two years ago."

"How was the county time?"

"It was okay, except they don't feed you very good. The fed is a lot better. They have bacon, eggs, sausage, and steak. You can take as much as you want, put five trays under your bed if you want to. You just can't have any moldy food there. They don't like that."

Now he has me a bit confused, because he could only know what he told me if he has served time in a federal penitentiary. Therefore, I ask him, "You spent time in a federal pen?"

"Yeah, one year."

"What was that for?"

"Possession of a firearm. My daddy gave me a pistol and told me I would be all right with it as long as I kept it in my suitcase. He never gave me any bad advice before, so I did what he said. I was on this bus, and the cops stopped and searched the entire bus and everyone on it. They found the pistol, and I got a year in the federal penitentiary in Oklahoma."

"You've just had those two years?"

"Yeah, but I've had lots of other time here and there, like six months, a week, two months."

"Were you raised in South Carolina?" I say, moving the conversation in a different direction.

"No, I'm from Maine. My mom still lives there."

"No dad?"

"A stepdad, but I call him Dad. He is my dad."

"What about your real dad?"

"I was supposed to meet him, but he was killed two weeks before that could happen, and that was that."

"How old were you?"

"Seventeen," he replies and surprises me with "You ever heard the expression, 'greasy grizzly'?" Apparently, mentioning Maine triggered old memories and associations.

"Uh, no, I haven't," I answer matter-of-factly.

"Well, big old grizzlies are real nasty. When they kill something, they roll in it and get the guts and blood matted in their coat, which gets really greasy and full of maggots. It's bad, man. They just get that stuff in their hair, and they smell, and they have all those maggots on them. That's why they are called greasy grizzlies," he says, obviously pleased with his remark.

Now he moves to the other side, but I don't follow him, supposing I have asked him enough. He swipes at the rest of the chrome, but none of the work on my eight-year-old truck has been easy, and I can tell he is not up to the job.

"You really need a high-speed buffer, man," I hear him say to me below the driver's window.

"Let me take a look," I reply, already knowing what I will find.

He has sort of done it and sort of hasn't.

"That's okay," I tell him. "The truck has over a million miles on it, and I don't expect perfection." I hand him a twenty-dollar bill.

"If you ever need anything, man, my handle is Static. You want women, drugs, or anything, I can get it for you. Drivers come to me when they want something. Just ask for Static on the CB."

"Okay," I answer, knowing I never would, even if I had a CB.

"Catch you later, man," Steve says, grabbing his bag. He walks off across the parking lot toward the motel where I see him stop another man crossing his path. They speak for a moment before parting, and Steve disappears around the corner of the motel where I first saw him.

THEY DANCE

At a Phoenix, Arizona, Wendy's restaurant, the side door next to the service window opens, and a young couple in their twenties enters. A small-breasted woman and a muscular man, both nearly six feet tall, they're rather attractive. He sports a goatee and a buzz cut and wears, tucked into black jeans, a dark-blue velour sweatshirt with a black-trimmed collar. Her sunglasses sit perched atop her light-brown teased and curled hair that falls just below her shoulders. She wears a loose white sweatshirt over a white blouse, and her jeans fit, but aren't tight.

As they enter the restaurant, they walk close together. In the ordering line, they stand, touching, with their backs to me. As I watch, he fondly slips his hand onto her left butt cheek. Almost immediately, her hand slips down and around to grasp his hand in her own, and they hold hands as they continue to study the menu. In a moment, distracted, she releases his hand, which again slips around to her butt cheek. Without speaking, for she doesn't say "No" or "Stop that," she just again takes his hand and removes it from her butt. When she does this, I laugh a short, spontaneous laugh no one notices.

Finally, the couple orders and afterward settles into a four-chair table. Sitting at opposite corners, she at the window and he next to the aisle, their faces express playful jostling. Still, their steadfast independence is obvious and says about her and him, "Many men want me, many women want me." This delicate balance moves back and forth like a dance, a circling, smiling, teasing dance.

SOMEONE STILL CARES

On a sunny afternoon, a car a ways ahead of me on busy I-15 north of Phoenix, Arizona, pulls onto the shoulder and stops. A door opens and a slender, hip-looking young woman emerges carrying a small bunch of long-stemmed flowers in her right hand. With brisk determination, she strides toward a two-foot cross, inscribed with JOSH. *Well, Josh, someone still cares.*

People do this everywhere, put up these road markers, death markers. I don't know if this one is still there, because I think road crews remove them after a while.

INDOMITABLE

As a relief from trucking after three months on the road, I stop in Tucson, Arizona, to visit some friends. One morning, awakening to a quiet house, I decide on a walk. Outside, a cornucopia of desert vegetation borders the sandy, narrow driveway, for my friends live on five acres. Half-asleep, I follow the driveway, ambling unhurriedly, enjoying the tranquility interwoven with the soft calls of doves.

Beneath my feet, tire tracks in the sand crisscross in a rippled, uneven pattern. Studying the pattern, I see a black ant, perhaps a half-inch long, struggling to carry a piece of reddish desert debris, possibly a fragment of a prickly pear cactus. Bending down over him, I watch as he tries to climb a tire ridge that for him is a wall. The piece he carries outweighs him, and he easily topples over, tumbling down into the groove as though the bit carries him instead. Yet he persists, righting himself, and again climbs the ridge. This time he manages to push over the top and trudge on, his heavy load swinging him around like a pendulum and causing him to travel in a jagged circle, like a punch-drunk clown. Tenaciously clutching his prize, he tips over, standing on his head with his legs churning in the air, and I laugh. Falling sideways, he regains his stance and again marches on, never stopping, never giving up, stubbornly determined, indomitable.

When I die, I'm coming back as an ant. So watch out, world!

OUT OF THE SKY

The song "Fire and Rain" fills the cab of my truck as I listen to "Spotlight on James Taylor" on the radio. With Taylor's serenade, I drive west on I-10 near Lordsburg, New Mexico. Vast open desert surrounds me, and distant mountains with darkly rugged peaks, some pointed, some rounded, run together into massive ridges. Layered, gray clouds cover the sky, and from them a few scattered, dark bands reach the ground, rain pouring out of the sky like the gushing stream from a tipped bucket of water. As I travel on, the road changes direction every few miles until ahead, a burst of rain straddles the highway. Quickly approaching, I drive into a torrent of water that pounds the windshield. Startled, I abruptly slow as the downpour floods the road. Plowing through the water, I worry the truck will hydroplane, and the wind will push me into the ditch. Gradually, the rain slows and stops as I drive from under the bursting cloud into the sunshine.

Scanning ahead, I see, not surprisingly, another dark band. Yet this one looks different, and I recognize a whirling mass of dust. The whirling funnel turns and bends across the desert, fast approaching my truck. Perhaps it will miss me. But it hits and engulfs the truck cab in swirling dust and bits of straw and other debris, rattling and rocking the truck. Seconds later, the funnel whirls away, and I watch it blow out and disappear into the air. Now there are only one or two faint, distant bands marking the sky as Taylor's soothing voice resonates around me singing, "You've got a friend."

This was so cool, first the rain and then the dust. It makes me wonder how this could happen. How was it that the rain cloud was where it was just as I passed through, and then the dust funnel found me only to blow through and disappear?

YOU AREN'T GOING TO DRINK THAT THEN DRIVE, ARE YOU, DRIVER?

At Laredo, Texas, cross-border commerce slows in January and February. On the last Saturday in February, I sit at the Pilot Truck Stop, parked since Friday, because my load doesn't deliver in Laredo until Monday morning. Thus, I wander in and out of the convenience store between stints of writing to get out of the truck and to spark up with a hotdog or a sandwich. As I leave the store on one such excursion, I see a driver in front of me carrying a small brown bag, the size used for a single can of beer, and I am concerned, wondering if he intends to drink that and then drive.

As I watch, he climbs into his truck and exits the fuel island, stopping briefly to chug the can, which he then tosses into the trash, still in the paper bag, and drives off. Recovering the discarded can to confirm my fears, I take it out of the bag. Hmmm.

I find an empty can of a French vanilla diet drink. Well, he was rather fat!

WHAT WORDS SOFTLY

In southern Texas, driving on a two-lane road, I pass through mostly dry, dusty country. Yet ahead I see an unexpected oasis of lush vegetation and think there must be a river there. Reaching a bridge, I start across and look down to a pool below. There a young couple stands close together in chest-high water, for the pleasant summer day is a good time for a swim. He holds her in his arms, and as they look into each other's eyes, who knows what words softly float between them?

TRY ANOTHER DAY

Fifteen miles north of Laredo, Texas, at a border patrol checkpoint on I-35, the traffic separates into auto and truck lanes. I move right into the truck lane and stop where an officer waits. When I roll down the window, he asks, "Are you an American citizen?"

"Yes," I say. Meanwhile a second officer with a German shepherd patrols around my truck, sniffing for humans and drugs.

"Is anyone in the truck with you?" he asks.

"No," I tell him as the other officer and his canine partner complete their inspection.

"Have a nice day," the first officer says, stepping back and allowing me to continue.

As I roll forward, passing the office, I happen to look left and see a parked car with an open trunk. Inside a man quietly lies curled up, his eyes open and alert. I think he is an illegal immigrant from Mexico or South America. Now caught, the border patrol will bus him back to Mexico where he will try another day to get to America.

Imagine living in poverty and wanting a better life for yourself. What would you do to get it?

LIKE PART OF THE EARTH IT WILL SOON BECOME

The flat highway crossing the Oklahoma prairie stretches out before me. Overhead, a gray expanse of clouds blankets the sky and permeates the air, the gloomy day suitable for a funeral. As the open and seemingly endless land streams by my windows, I spot a lifeless coyote ahead, stretched flat and motionless on the shoulder of the highway. Yet its fur ruffles in the wind, mimicking the prairie grass, the body already looking like part of the earth it will soon become.

MOONLIGHT MISHAP

As I wait for a new trip assignment at our Laredo, Texas, terminal, warm air breezes through the open truck windows, soothing me as my mind lazily drifts. Then the Qualcomm erupts with a droning buzz, disrupting my reverie. Reaching for the smaller-than-laptop-size keyboard, I settle it in front of me on the steering wheel and press the READ NEXT button. The trip information appears on the screen, and I scroll down the page, picking out bits and pieces of relevant information. The load is paint, a hazardous material, headed to a North Carolina truck manufacturer; it is heavy, waits at the terminal, and doesn't have a delivery appointment.

Bobtailing through the yard, I locate and hook up to the trailer. Back in the cab, I send in the load-up message, accepting the load. Because the load is heavy, it has to be weighed, so I drive the three blocks to the Pilot Truck Stop, weigh on the CAT scale, and find all three axles legal. Afterward, I go to the restaurant for a sandwich.

When I return to the truck, the Qualcomm buzzes with two messages. The first one, the delivery appointment, surprises me, because the appointment is for yesterday. The second message is from a supervisor who curtly demands, "Why aren't you driving? This load is late, and if you didn't think you could deliver it on time, you shouldn't have accepted it."

Blood flushes my face as I think, *What an asshole.* Someone deliberately omitted the delivery appointment until I accepted the load, and that pisses me off. I shoot back an angry reply, even though I know the supervisor won't receive it, because my messages go to my fleet manager. Still, I accepted the load, so I must deliver it.

Before I can leave, dispatch sends a message to swap with another truck about halfway to Houston on US Route 59, a secondary and mostly two-lane road. Otherwise, I would travel I-35 north to San Antonio and turn east on I-10 to Houston. Instead I start east on Route 59. But before driving far, I receive another message telling me to swap the load at our Houston drop yard. About halfway to Houston I pass the first swap driver, and we wave. Route 59 has rough patches and is even worse at railroad crossings, and though I slow down at them, the trailer jumps.

On reaching our Houston drop yard about midnight, I turn right into a wide, half-mile-long driveway that also services other businesses. Halfway down I see a sign reading SPEED BUMP, and so I slow and meet a small bump. Relaxing, I continue faster until *wham*, I hit the actual speed bump. The trailer jumps and slams down hard onto the blacktop. I wince. I enter the yard, park and, after unhooking, walk to the rear of the trailer to check the seal. What I see startles me. White paint seeps from the bottom of the trailer doors and from cracks on the sides and floor underneath. *What the hell?* Now, despairingly, I know I cannot swap the load.

Back in the cab, I send off a message describing the problem and afterward call our safety hotline. The safety supervisor tells me to open and enter the trailer. If I find spillage, I must buy an absorbent, possibly kitty litter, to soak it up. When I open the trailer, paint fumes spill out, and as I climb up into the trailer, suffocating fumes sting my eyes and overwhelm me, causing me to gasp. Stumbling back, I desperately flail about in the dark for any handhold. Just before falling backward into space, I manage to grab the edge of a hinge and catch myself. Awkwardly I climb to the ground, where I struggle for air before gradually returning to normal. Afterward I again call safety and again the officer tells me to enter the trailer and check on the spill. When I tell him about the fumes, he says to wait until they clear out.

I decide I might as well search for kitty litter. Because I am unfamiliar with Houston, however, I don't know where I might find a store open at one o'clock in the morning. Leaving the trailer at the yard, I start driving and about two miles away find a twenty-four-hour convenience store that has three small bags of kitty litter. I buy them, although I am skeptical they will be of much use.

When I return to the yard, I check the trailer, and the fumes are still too strong. I wait another hour before checking again. This time, though the fumes still affect my breathing, I impatiently decide to push ahead. Once inside I shine my flashlight around and discover six round containers that are four feet in diameter and four feet tall. Three containers stand in front and three in back, spread across the width of the trailer, with the outside containers placed close to the sidewalls. There is a tight space for me to squeeze through, and as I do, paint smears on my clothes, for white paint covers the rear three containers and most of the floor.

On searching for the source of the leak with my flashlight, I find a large circular spot on the ceiling above one of the rear containers and, on checking that container, I see a hole in the top center with a missing two-inch plug. I am incredulous. I cannot believe all this paint came from that two-inch hole. Half jokingly, I spread out the kitty litter, which works like putting a sponge into a bathtub full of water. Squeezing around the containers to scatter the litter, I smear paint on my hands, clothes, and shoes. Soon I'm a mess.

Tired, and weakened by the fumes, I climb out of the trailer. The night's warm air envelops me, and I gaze up at the stars for a moment before removing my clothes to discover white spots on my arms and legs where the paint soaked through. Standing nearly naked in the moonlight, I try to wipe the paint off my skin as best I can. But the paint doesn't come off. Disheartened, I give up trying. Still, I tell myself, *This will all be over tomorrow—or perhaps the next day—but it will pass.*

Back in the cab, I again call safety to tell them I cannot stop the leaking and that I am going to bed. I hope the paint will dry up by morning. In the morning when I awaken, I unhappily find smeared paint on the steering wheel, seat, and floor of the cab. I will have to clean that up later, because first I must check on the trailer. Walking around to the back and peering into the trailer, I discover the paint is still wet, and I am disappointed. As I inspect the dripping paint, another driver, obviously curious, approaches me.

"This is quite a mess you have here," he says, noting the spilled paint in the trailer.

"Yes, it is," I agree. "I was hoping it would dry up by this morning, but obviously it hasn't."

"That will never dry up," he tells me, "because they don't put any fixative in it."

After he leaves, I return to the cab where I find a message to call the account manager. When she answers, I say, "Hi, this is 5382 (my truck number). You wanted me to call?"

"Yes. We need to get that load moving. What is your estimated delivery time?" she asks.

"This is a leaking hazmat load," I explain to her. "I don't know when I can deliver it."

"You have to get moving because the consignee needs that load," she says firmly. "What is your estimated time of arrival at the consignee?" she again asks.

"This is a hazmat load, and it is leaking," I repeat to her. "That is very serious. There is no way I am taking this trailer out onto the highway in this condition."

"We have to get that load moving," she again says. "I will get back to you."

Soon I receive another message to call the safety coordinator, which I do.

"What is the status of that load? Is it still leaking?" he asks.

"Well, I am on my cell phone, so let me go out and look." Outside I kneel down beside the trailer and tell him, "Yes, it is still dripping, and I won't take this trailer out on the highway like this."

To my ecstatic relief, he says, "I am taking you off this load. You will shortly receive a message from your fleet manager."

"Okay," I reply. Hanging up, I rejoice with "Hallelujah!" Directly, I receive the message "You are off load." Dispatch assigns me a shag load, which takes until late afternoon to deliver. When I return to the drop yard, the paint trailer is gone. Now how do you suppose they did that?

IT IS NOT SO GOOD ANYMORE

At 6:00 p.m., I arrive at Clampett Paper in San Antonio, Texas, for an appointment tomorrow morning at 8:00 a.m. I will sleep here overnight. A sign on the Clampett Paper end of the building proclaiming Vacancies puzzles me. I check the bills and discover a different address, though looking further, I find both addresses on the packing list. Still, I worry Clampett Paper may have moved. Walking around front to check, I find picture windows through which I see dozens of shelves of paper. So they haven't moved. They must have two locations. Yes, but which one am I supposed to deliver to? There's nothing more I can do now, so I may as well go to bed.

I wake up at seven o'clock, dress, and go inside. A man restocking shelves tells me, "The receiver should arrive in about fifteen minutes." So I return to my truck. Although I know which dock they use, I don't back in because of my doubt about the address. As I wait, another truck approaches, and I watch him, hoping he drives by. Instead he backs into the open dock, blocking me out. This angers me, but I decide he probably only has a few skids like me, so unloading shouldn't take long.

When the receiver arrives, he agrees to take my entire load, even though three pallets belong at their other location. Yet, of course, first he must unload the other truck already in the dock. When he opens the dock door and drops the plate into the trailer, the other driver comes in with his bills. When I peer into his trailer, I only see six skids. During the unloading, the other driver looks guiltily at me, obviously aware of what he did.

"I am sorry I got in front of you," he says apologetically, with a heavy accent. His easy, considerate manner disarms me.

"I was pissed off at first, but now it's okay," I tell him. "I see you only have a few skids, so it won't take long. Besides, I wasn't sure of the address. I thought I might have to go to their other location."

"Do you have a trailer load?" he asks me.

"No, just a few skids like you," I say. Because I am curious about his accent, I push the conversation forward. "We are lucky to still have such nice weather in October."

"I just came from Chicago, and it is raining there," he says.

"Well, at least it isn't the white stuff," I counter.

"No, no, not that," he affirms.

"Do you drive forty-eight states?" I ask him.

"No, just up to Chicago and the states between here and there," he says. "Did you know they are raising the toll in Chicago from one twenty-five to four dollars on January first? That is over 300 percent," he says. "It is nuts."

He means the toll for each toll stop and, if headed toward western Wisconsin, there are eight toll stops, for a total cost of thirty-two dollars instead of the usual ten dollars. "They raised the tolls in Ohio and Pennsylvania, too," I tell him, "and my company doesn't want to pay it, so it makes us use secondary roads."

"You are a company man?" he asks, glancing at my truck.

"No, I bought this truck from the company, which is why it looks like a company truck. I am an owner-operator leased back to them. Are you a company driver?" I ask him.

"It is my truck," he says, "but I am unhappy about it now. It is so expensive. All of my friends have sold their trucks. When I started, fuel was a dollar. Now it is so much more, and I don't earn any more per mile. I just bought eight new tires for $3,100. It is the same with everything. It is not so good anymore," he says, and I understand he isn't just talking about trucking.

He continues, "I pay $7,500 in property taxes. My friend pays $10,000. My Social Security benefit is only $500, and I pay and pay Social Security, but it is bad. It may go bankrupt," he says and shrugs.

"You have Social Security now?" I question him.

"No, no, when I retire, but it is nothing, and I cannot retire until sixty-five. By then they may raise it to sixty-eight or sixty-nine. In Europe, you retire at fifty-five or in some countries fifty-seven. To wait to sixty-five is ten more years. Many people don't live that long. My friend died at fifty-five. He had cancer."

"How old are you?" I ask.

"Fifty," he says.

I see a stocky, healthy-looking man whose hair is only just beginning to gray. "You have a strong accent. What is that?" I say to him.

"I am from Poland. I came over in 1968," he states.

"You're a citizen, or how does that work?" I ask.

"You have a 'green card' and after four years become a citizen. I am a citizen of two countries," he says proudly, "but it is not so good here anymore. I may go back to Poland when I retire."

"It won't be the same," I tell him. "It will have changed."

He just shrugs. "It is getting worse here. Who knows what will happen? It just keeps getting worse."

When he says this, I believe he is right, and so I say insincerely, "Maybe I should go to Poland, too."

He lowers his head, and because of this I cannot hear his reply, but I believe he says, "You belong here."

"Do you have family?" I ask.

"Yes, a wife and daughter," he confirms.

I wonder, but don't ask, how they feel about returning to Poland. Instead I say, "Where do you live?"

"I live here," he says, meaning San Antonio.

The receiver finishes unloading and hands the driver his bills. They exchange parting words, and the driver turns to leave, but not before reaching for my hand. We shake as he says, "It was nice to meet you."

"Yes," I say, "I enjoyed talking to you." As the door closes behind him, I wonder if he will return to Poland.

OUCH!

At our Dallas, Texas, terminal, three other drivers and I sit talking outside at a picnic table under an awning. One driver tells about using a quart juice bottle for his personal toilet. Those bottles do work well, for they have a twist-on cap, reseal, and won't spill. You can empty and reuse them, and they store easily in the space at the end of the bed. Still, the driver complained that after a while the bottles smell. Another driver interrupted to say he rinsed his out with bleach. That worked great, he told us, except the next time he used the bottle, the bleach got on his penis and burned the hell out of it.

I laughed my head off.

PUMPS

At 10:00 a.m., I arrive at the TA Truck Stop in Oklahoma City to park and await my new load assignment after having just split a load at our nearby drop yard. Backing in beside a J. B. Hunt, I see the driver talking on his CB radio. I park and set my brakes. A woman climbs into the Hunt truck through the passenger door. She is short, stocky, about forty, and fair-looking, probably the driver's wife. She gets in, and I see the driver put up the privacy curtains around the windows. A few moments later, the truck begins rocking. Hmm, okay, well, perhaps it isn't his wife. Five minutes later, the rocking stops, the door opens, and she climbs out and walks to another truck that just parked and climbs into that truck. There she goes back into the sleeper. The driver closes the curtains, and now that truck rocks. Five minutes pass and she gets out and walks to a third truck. She stands on the truck step, talking to the driver, but steps down as he opens the door, and in she goes. Shortly, that truck starts rocking.

Finally, bored with watching, I leave to buy something at the truck stop convenience store. When I come out of the store, she walks toward me across the parking lot. She says something I cannot hear. I just wave her on, and she spots another driver who just got out of his truck. She speaks to him for a moment, but they quickly separate, and she disappears down a row of trucks. I don't know how many she does in an hour, but she just pumps right along.

In over ten years of driving, I only encountered prostitutes three or four times.

SWEET SALVATION

As I travel north on Wyoming Highway 85, a winding, narrow, two-lane road without a shoulder, the matte-gray February sky threatens a storm. Now, though, there are just powerful gusts of wind punching my empty trailer. I fight it, repeatedly adjusting the steering to stay in the lane. A fierce gust slams the truck, the wind pushing the top of the trailer sideways. The trailer tilts and twists until the rear wheels on the driver's side lift a couple feet off the road as I watch them in the mirror. *Is it going over?* I wonder. I jockey the steering with sharp, short turns back and forth, snaking the tractor trailer to try to bring the wheels down. The wheels hang suspended in the air one second…two seconds. I watch anxiously. Then the wheels drop, *bam*, onto the asphalt. Yet another gust slams the trailer, and again the trailer tilts, the wheels lifting. I fight the wind until again, *bam*, the trailer drops. For the third time, again the trailer tilts and lifts. It hangs there two or three seconds, threatening to flop over and ram the tractor down onto the passenger side. Instead, for the third time, the wheels slam onto the asphalt.

Finally the road turns, angling east. The wind persists, mile after mile, roughly shaking the trailer and keeping me on edge, pumped with adrenaline. I drive on, keenly aware the next gust could topple the truck. After an hour of agonizing driving, I finally reach Torrington, Wyoming, and my customer, a beet-sugar mill. With relief I turn into its yard, knowing if the wind doesn't stop before I leave, the slamming gusts will no longer matter. That's because a load of beet sugar, my sweet salvation, weighs forty-five thousand pounds, and the wind cannot blow the truck over with that in the trailer.

This was scary as hell! When the trailer lifts and tilts like that, at first the tractor stays flat, and if you aren't looking in the mirror, you don't realize the trailer is tilting. As the trailer lifts and continues, the key is whether or not it reaches its center of gravity, when more weight passes from one side of the center to the other. Once the trailer lifts and passes that point, it won't come back. It will continue lifting and pulling the tractor with it, and you're gone.

SAFETY GLASS

I am in the Chicago area for a morning delivery, driving down one of the many secondary highways that crisscross adjoining residential and commercial suburban neighborhoods. The streets are wet from a recent storm, and the cloudy sky threatens more rain. As I travel down the street, my tires kick up water left on the asphalt and spray a mist out behind me.

Suddenly, *Wham*, a mud ball slams into the windshield in front of my face. I cry out, "Whoa," as the windshield cracks into a maze of jagged, intersecting lines. Mud and cracks sharply reduce my visibility, and, unnerved, I brake. Straining to see through the splattered mud and splintered glass, I fear the closeness of cars. Slowing down, I bear right onto the shoulder where I stop after a hundred feet or so. Sitting there for a moment, I just stare at the mud and cracked window.

I exit the cab and look for the culprit. I focus on a wooded lot on the right side of the road; however, I don't see anyone. Climbing onto the hood, I scrape off the mud with a window squeegee, and the damage amazes me. The entire driver's window panel has cracked a hundred different ways yet, fortunately, remains firmly in place, an affirmation of the name "safety glass."

This makes me remember a story told to me by another driver. On Halloween some years past, someone dropped a pumpkin from an interstate highway overpass that smashed through the window of a tractor trailer and killed the driver. It's the same as if the truck sat parked and the pumpkin hit the glass at sixty-five miles an hour. The pumpkin didn't break. Even the best safety glass couldn't stop that.

PAPER WOMAN

With the engine shut off and no other trucks nearby, a quiet and peaceful aura surrounds me. I lie stripped and uncovered on my bed on a warm August night. The temperature is comfortable enough to sleep, yet I cannot. The busy, stressful day tensed my muscles, and I cannot relax, but I know something that helps.

Stretching my arm back past my head to the top left-hand corner of the bed, I grasp a partly used roll of paper towels, the size just fitting my hand. Reaching across my body, I begin to smoothly rub my limp other hand—the palm, the fingers—and gradually work up my arm as I feel the soft stroking relaxing my nerves. I move the roll over my shoulder to cross my chest, back and forth, lower and lower to my stomach. There I switch hands, again starting with my palm. Slowly, moving in a sensual, caressing motion up my other arm, the soft, pliant paper glides on my skin. At my shoulder I lift the roll and guide it around the contours of my face, the forehead and cheeks, in a way vaguely reminiscent of what a woman might do with her hands.

Then sitting up and bending my leg, I manage to massage my left foot—the bottom, sides, and top. Continuing up my leg, I turn sideways to reach the thick, resistant muscles while feeling the tension releasing, my buzzing, irritated nerves quieting. With more bends and turns, I rub my other foot and leg, my buttocks, and parts of my back. Finally, I return the paper towels to the corner of the bed. As I serenely lie there in the warm dark air, drowsiness settles on me like downy feathers, and I can't remember falling asleep.

Paper towels will never be the same again. I can see it now; there will be a run on stores. Ha!

JUST AS BETTY SAID

Near Philadelphia, Pennsylvania, a phone rings, and a droning voice answers, "Blake Anderson Company" (not their name).

"Hi, this is a driver, and I need directions. I am coming north on Highway 202 from Delaware."

"Two-oh-two?" she asks.

"Yes," I say.

"Well, take exit six and turn right to the first left. There is a Ford dealership there. Take that to the end and turn right. We're the second driveway on the left."

"Are you sure I turn right off 202?"

"Yes," she confirms.

"I will be going east," I say.

"Yes, I suppose so. I don't really know my east or west, but I am certain you turn right," she says decisively.

In the morning, I take exit six and turn right to the first left, as Betty directed. However, to my dismay, I don't find a Ford dealership there. Instead, homes and parked cars line a dead-end street, and I know I've turned the wrong way. I should have turned left. Now I am in trouble.

Stopping, I look into my rearview mirror and count a half dozen cars behind me. I cannot turn around or back up. Ahead, the narrow road passes through a tunnel of overhanging tree branches before bending right out of sight. A heavy knot settles in my gut, a building panic as I face the only possibility. Turning on my four-way flashers, I slowly drive forward as tree branches bang, dig, and scrape on the top and passenger side of the trailer. Some of them make popping noises as they break, and I hope they don't fall on the cars behind me. Steering down the center of the road, most of the noise stops.

After about a mile I again stop, for I need to find out what lies ahead. Climbing out of my cab, I walk back to the car following me, and a middle-aged man lowers his window.

"Hi, I'm lost," I say to him. "I made a wrong turn and don't know where this road goes or how to get out of here. Can you help me, please?"

"Where are you trying to go?" he asks.

"I think I should have turned left off 202 instead of right, so I have to turn around."

"Hmm, well, a school up ahead has a turnaround. Follow me, and I will take you there."

A half mile farther, the driver stops at a driveway, waves, and goes on. The driveway leads steeply up between two pillars with meticulously landscaped flowerbeds. It is the entrance to a private school with ivy-covered buildings and manicured lawns, no place for a huge, hulking tractor trailer. *Oh, brother, I can't go in there.* Turning and looking down the road, I see a low underpass. *Oh no, now what do I do?*

Unhappily, I consider the driveway and think, *I could easily take out a flowerbed or a pillar, but what choice do I have? Okay, here goes.*

Starting in the lowest gear, I swing far wide right before cutting back and carefully beginning the turn up the grade. As I inch up the steep incline, dragging the heavily loaded trailer, the tractor lurches and jerks from the strain, bouncing me up and down in the seat. Nervously easing up the driveway, I watch the driver's side rear wheels edge within a couple of inches of the flowerbed and gate pillar, while the turning arch of the tractor trailer blocks the passenger-side view and any problem there. Anxiously I keep moving, jerking, jumping, and praying I don't hit anything. Finally I can straighten and pull up the driveway past the entrance, where I stop. "Whoa," I moan as I exit the truck to check the flowerbeds and pillars, which to my relief are fine. Looking around, I don't see the turnaround my helper mentioned, so when a bookish-looking boy in a car comes down the driveway, I stop him.

"There is supposed to be a turnaround here somewhere," I say to him.

"There is, but I don't think you can get around it." He tells me how to find it and leaves.

Walking up the driveway crossing green spacious lawn, I look for the turnaround. In front of a building I discover a tight circle hardly suitable for cars. *Oh, brother, now what do I do?* Returning to my truck, I realize I have one option and so continue forward into the campus following the driveway until, turning a corner, I find the driveway splits. Again I don't know what to do, so I stop. As I ponder the problem, doors open and dozens of teenagers, mostly girls, emerge from the buildings. They stroll along in groups of four or five, laughing and chatting nonstop, none of them noticing me. Leaning out my cab window, I call out to the nearest ones, "Excuse me," and again louder, "Excuse me." As they turn to me, I ask, "Could you please tell me how I can get out of here?"

Each of them looks at my truck and me until one responds, "Well, you could go down that way," and she points to the right. Then she qualifies her suggestion by adding, "But I don't know if you can make it around the corner down there."

"What about the other way?"

She hesitates before saying, "Yes, you could go that way."

"Are there any low trees or wires or anything else I might hit?"

She hesitates again but says, "No, I don't think so."

"And will that get me off the campus?"

"Yes, it will," she says.

"Thank you," I tell her.

She smiles before again taking up her chatter and walking on with her friends. After the last of them disappears inside the stately old buildings, I complete the turn. Soon, reaching the exit, I again face choices: turn left or right on the road confronting me or take the road opposite the campus driveway. I don't know what to do. As I sit there perplexed, a car happens along from the right. Determined to stop it, I hurriedly climb from the cab and, stepping into the car's path, force the driver to stop.

He lowers his window, and I approach him. "Hi. I'm lost and not supposed to be here. I took a wrong turn and don't know how to get out of here. Could you please help me?"

"Where do you want to go?" he asks.

"I came in on the road on the other side of the campus from Highway 202. I want to return there," I tell him.

"You could go that way"—he points the way he just came from—"but I don't know if you can make it around the corner down there."

I don't say it but suspect that way also leads to the low underpass. I ask him about the other way, and he responds, "Well, there is a small bridge that way, which I don't think you can cross."

Small bridge, low underpass, drooping tree branches, manicured lawns and flowerbeds, pillars, and too-tight turnarounds, and I'm still not out of trouble. At least I haven't hit a dead end yet. "What about the road over there," I ask apprehensively, referring to the opposite street. If it won't work, I'm in big trouble.

"That would be far out of your way," he replies.

"That's okay. Are there any low tree branches or anything else that might present a problem?"

"You should be able to clear the trees all right. That road ends, and you'll have to turn onto another street, but it's wide. Afterward you'll come to a highway where you turn left and after a couple of miles, you'll reach 202, but it is all marked," he explains. "Why don't you just follow me?"

"Thank you, that's very kind of you."

He starts, and I follow, again traveling the center of the road to avoid branches. Soon we reach the end and the left turn, which is easy, and after another mile, the highway. Here my guide leaves me. Shortly I find 202, this time heading south, the way Betty surely comes to work every day. Turning right at exit six to the first left, I happily see the Ford dealership. Taking the street to the end, I turn right to the second driveway on the left and, just as Betty said, there they are.

This was a nightmare!

HOW NOT TO SAY NO

On a rainy evening at a truck stop east of Knoxville, Tennessee, I haven't yet put up the curtain that wraps around in front of my windows. With three lights on inside the cab, anyone who cares to can easily see me. Though I'm aware of this, it doesn't bother me, because I sit writing on my computer, engrossed in a story. Because of this, I only vaguely hear a soft noise over the truck engine's invasive rumble. I hear the noise again and recognize that someone's knocking on the driver's side door.

Rising from the folding chair pressed against my bunk, I lean forward and across the driver's seat. Peering out the window, I see a young woman with an old face, staring up at me in the rain. She isn't wearing a hat or coat, and her wet clothes hang limply on her. When I roll down the window, she says something I cannot hear.

"What?" I question. She repeats her entreaty in a soft voice like her knock, and still I don't understand. "What is it you want?" I ask again.

Climbing up onto the step and hanging onto the window, she says, "Is there something I can do for money?"

When she says this, I sense she doesn't want to do anything, not sex, not polish my chrome wheels, not anything. Therefore, I reply by saying, "You want money?"

"Yes."

Reaching for my wallet, I take out two dollars and hand it to her.

"God bless you." She steps down and walks away, smiling.

As I watch her leave, I think, *I got off easy. Perhaps I should close the curtain, even though I do know how to say no.*

SLIP SLIDE AWAY

Just west of Flagstaff, Arizona, dense gray clouds blanket the winter night sky, blocking the moon and stars. Last night a storm dropped six or so inches of heavy, wet snow. Though the warmer day and heavy use melted down the interstate's right lane to bare blacktop, ice and packed snow cover the left lane. At fifty-five miles an hour, I haven't overtaken any cars or trucks, and none have passed.

However, in my mirrors I see another tractor trailer quickly closing the gap between us. As his headlights grow brighter, I think he must be doing at least seventy, the posted limit. In moments he is on me, not slowing and moving left onto the icy blacktop. He starts to pass but falters beside me, matching my speed, for I guess the icy road surprised him. Though he cannot hear me, I call out, "Don't stop there, Buddy, keep moving and keep passing." He doesn't, and his truck begins to edge sideways. He works to recover and does as we barrel down the highway through the darkness side by side.

Then, again, his truck slips. This time it slides even farther left; now he's driving on the edge of the shoulder. I watch for him to come back. Instead he slips farther until the driver's side tires drop off the hard pavement onto the softer lower shoulder. The tractor trailer tilts and begins slip sliding sideways down the bank. It plunges forward through the snow and throws spray off both sides. I wonder if it will roll, tumbling in an awkward flip-flop down the bank. Yet he manages to keep it upright to the median's flat bottom where it slows to a stop as I fly past and on down the highway.

I suffer guilt from this story. It's the old hindsight. I could have cut my speed so he could have gotten over. It just didn't occur to me at the time. Sorry!

SHAKING

At the Jessup, Maryland, TA near Baltimore, I slowly drive around the large parking lot. I am there to swap my empty with another driver for his multiple stop construction-site load. Searching among more than one hundred spaces, now nearly full, I find the dropped trailer parked beside a bobtail. Seeing me, the driver emerges from his cab with the bill of lading in his hand, and I roll down the window to receive it. He hands it up to me.

"What are you hauling?" he asks.

"Actually, I just have an empty."

"Oh, well, that's okay," he says, sounding relieved.

Sensing this, I ask, "How long have you been driving?"

"I just finished training last week. This is my first load," he tells me.

I think, *What a dumb-ass thing for dispatch to do, giving him a construction-site load, one of our toughest deliveries, for his first load.*

"I understand you couldn't find the Marine barracks," I carefully say without judgment, not wanting to offend him.

"No, I couldn't."

"What happened?"

Obviously embarrassed, he hesitates before answering. "I made the first delivery okay, but that was early in the morning. My second appointment was the Marine barracks at 10:00 a.m. As soon as I left the beltway, I got lost and found myself on a street where ahead I could see an underpass. Right away I worried, because from a distance it appeared too low. As I came closer, I looked for the usual numbers marking the height, but there weren't any, and so I just stopped, because close up the span looked even lower. What else could I do?" He had a pleading nervousness in his eyes that said he needed sympathy and support.

"You did right. That was the best thing you could have done. What happened then?"

"As I got out of the truck to check, I saw several cars stopped behind me. Looking at the bridge, I knew the trailer would hit it. I felt this knot well up in my stomach, because

I would have to back up. Fortunately, the cars blocked by my truck began passing, and soon the space behind me was clear. I hurriedly climbed into my truck, and with my flashers on, I blindly and slowly backed up the street the wrong way, scared to death I was going to hit somebody. I had to go three blocks before I could turn. It was awful, but that was only the beginning. "I turned down another street without any idea where I was going. After a few blocks, I had to turn again because of a No Trucks sign. Yet I was unable to get around the corner because of the narrow street and the cars parked on both sides. I needed to back up, so I could swing out into the oncoming lane to complete the turn but was again unable to do so because of the cars stopped behind me. This time I didn't get out immediately, because I was becoming increasingly upset.

"After what seemed like a long time, I did get out and talked to the driver behind me. When I told him what I needed to do, he agreed to move back and stay there while I turned. After backing up, I swung out to make the turn, but as I began turning, cars drove around the waiting car and shot past me on the right. Turning into the narrow street, I closed the gap and began edging between the parked cars, desperately hoping I wouldn't hit anything and no one would hit me. Finally, I cleared everything, completing the turn by bringing the tractor in line with the trailer.

"However, I was still lost and had no idea what was ahead. Soon I was in downtown Washington and expecting the police to pull me over and ticket me, but I never saw any police. Instead I kept going until I came to a wide, heavily traveled highway-numbered street, which I turned onto, thinking it might lead me back to the beltway, and it did." He pauses before saying, "I'm quitting. I called my dispatcher and asked to be routed back to the main terminal, so I can turn in my truck."

"What? No! No way, you are not quitting! It's always hard when you first start, just like any job," I tell him.

"Yes, but I didn't think it would be this hard. I was shaking," he said glumly.

"You're not the first one to do that. I've been there, too, but you can't quit. Don't you have a $3,000 loan to pay back for truck school? How will you pay that back without a job?

"You did everything right, except you didn't find the customer. You faced a low underpass, which you checked and realized was too low. You backed up three blocks without hitting anything. Most new drivers would have just hoped the underpass was high enough and kept going, only to slam into it, wrecking the trailer and possibly even becoming stuck under there. Likewise, on the tight corner you went around, where most new drivers would keep turning until they hit a pole or even a car. You were cautious and because of it, you didn't hit anything. In addition, you drove through DC without a ticket. I won't say you won't have more problems until you gain experience—you will—but you have common sense. Believe me, not every driver has that. You can do this."

"I don't know." He waffled. "I have to call my fleet manager," he said and left to use the truck stop's phone.

Fifteen minutes later, he returned, and I asked him, "Well, are you going to quit?"

"No, I guess not, but they are going to charge me for a late load."

"No problem. The company allows you three late loads in a year before they will fire you. You can do this," I tell him.

"I suppose so."

"No suppose about it. You can do it. It won't be easy, but you can do it, and this job, like any job, gets easier after a while."

"I have to go," he says, nervously shuffling his feet.

"Okay, well, good luck to you."

"Thanks," he replies before turning away to his truck. I watch him go, thinking, *If he just doesn't give up, he will be fine.*

BIG, DUMB, SLOW TRUCK—SMALL, SMART, FAST CAR

I need to shop, pick up a few groceries and miscellaneous items. Walmart is a good place to do that, because I can usually park there. But if the lot looks jammed, I pass. This time, however, as I scan a Walmart from the highway, I see room in the dock area on the end of the building. From a street alongside the parking lot, I pull in by the docks and look for the best place to park. I decide to back up to the building.

Curving around, I pull forward to get a straight back. In doing so, I block off the rear driveway leading to the front parking lot. Checking my mirrors and finding nothing behind me, I push back while continuing to watch my mirrors. When I am about ten feet from the wall, a car appears, cutting through.

"Damn!" My adrenaline jumps as I hit the brakes, jerking the truck and trailer in a short snap as the car barely slips through, and I am mad. "Son of a bitch," I call out. Watching the car park, I hurriedly climb out of my truck to reach the driver before he or she enters the building. A young woman emerges from the car and starts toward the store a few steps. When she sees me approaching, she stops, waiting. When I am close enough to her, I say sternly while controlling my anger, "I almost hit you, and I don't want to hit you. Don't do that again!"

"I'm sorry."

This sort of thing happens often, people getting impatient and not wanting to wait for a truck to get out of the way. Yes, I know it's a pain in the butt; however, you should wait, because you can never be absolutely sure what a truck will do, and often the driver can't see you. Give drivers a break. They aren't trying to inconvenience you. They are just trying to do their jobs.

I WORK HARD ENOUGH ALREADY

A patrol car's flashing red lights in my left mirrors grab my attention. Uh-oh! Glancing at my speedometer, I discover my speed is sixty-eight, barely over the limit. Well, I am not speeding, so what's the problem? As I stop on the shoulder, the worrisome lights keep flashing, and I cannot imagine what the problem might be. Stopping behind me, the officer exits his car and walks up alongside my truck to stand beneath my now open driver's window, where I expectantly wait.

"Let me see your logbook, please, driver," he politely commands me.

Reaching down into the pockets on the door panel, I pull out a logbook and start handing it to him when I realize I have the wrong one. "Oops, that's the wrong book." I replace it and give him the correct one. As he takes the logbook, I see his expression change to a frown, and I quickly realize why. He thinks he has caught me running two books, falsifying my hours to drive extra miles.

"Give me that other logbook also," he orders me rather sternly. I do, and he scans the second book, looking intently at the pages. That book is last month's log, which I haven't yet filed in the storage above the door. Checking my current log, he hands both logbooks back to me.

"Thank you, driver," he says and returns to his patrol car.

When he is gone, I engage the transmission and ease back out onto the highway, thinking, *I don't know how to run two logbooks. Besides, I work hard enough already and don't want to run any more miles.*

IN A SECOND OF SEEING

On the interstate in Ohio, while passing through lush woods and over a slip of a bridge, I happen to look right through the break in the foliage. Down below, walking across the shallow stream, two deer with regal antlers gracefully move through the shadows of overhanging trees and narrow shafts of light angling down from the sun.

I love this, capturing a moment. I'm amazed how things like this happen. A moment or two later and the deer might have been gone, or maybe I wouldn't have looked.

ACCIDENTAL SEDUCTION

The slight woman lithely scurries around the restaurant, busily taking and serving orders. Though, perhaps fifty or more years old, she is still attractive. As I watch her, she stops with her back to me, clearing a table, gathering the plates and silverware, and placing them in a plastic tub. As she removes the dirty dishes and wipes down the table, I notice her long, auburn hair, thick, with gray streaks. She has pinned it up in a bun, and I wonder what she would look like with it down. As I consider this, the hairpin holding her hair loosens, and her hair uncurls in a sensuous, magical motion. Down her back it falls to her waist where the thick braids seductively sway back and forth, riveting my attention. I sit transfixed as she reaches around, coiling her hair and securing it up with the pin. In a sideways glance, she sees me watching her and does a double take.

"Sometimes the pin doesn't hold," she says by way of explanation, suggesting her falling hair was accidental and not an attempt to seduce me. Now finished with the table, she hurries the dishes into the kitchen, and I watch her go.

It was incredible the way her hair fell and how it made me feel watching it fall to her waist.

IN A FLURRY OF WINGS

A strong, gusty wind rocks the trailer as I speed down the highway. Yet my heavy load keeps the truck hunkered down, and I only experience minor problems steadying it. Suddenly, a dove, tossed in the overpowering currents and fighting to right itself, flashes in a flurry of wings before my windshield. Though it misses the glass, disappearing up, I hear a thud as it smashes into the high-rise cab roof. Checking my mirrors, I watch for it behind me, and in an instant it appears rolling uncontrollably through the air and smacks the blacktop, tumbling three or four times before stopping, deathly still.

Wow! When something like this happens, I'm touched. I can't help it.

COVETING THE BEAUTIFUL

Returning to my truck after talking to a customer, I notice several embedded moths and a ragtag assortment of bugs on the bug screen snapped onto the truck's radiator. I know they will stay there until the wind blows them off or a jet of water at the truck wash scours them away. There aren't any butterflies. If there were, I would carefully remove them and save them in a see-through plastic container that once held hard-boiled eggs or some other deli food bought at a truck stop. I don't keep moths, because no one wants moths, for no one covets the ordinary.

Yet many people want the butterflies, the beautiful butterflies, and I give them to friends and even to strangers, like the small, modest woman fueling her car at a Flying J Truck Stop. I thought it likely she would have children and might want a swallowtail butterfly I recently collected. I was eager to give it away before the truck's vibrations damaged the butterfly's thin, translucent wings. When I approached her, she said yes, she did have children, and, yes, she would like to have the butterfly. She carefully took the plastic container from my hand and reverently placed it on the backseat of her car.

HOWDY, MA'AM, WOULD YOU LIKE TO DANCE?

While completing my bookwork in the driver's seat at a truck stop, a man and woman stand just to the left front of my truck, engaged in a conversation I cannot hear. Yet, watching them, I decide the woman wants something from the man. As he listens to her, he appears resistant, which convinces me that they are not a couple. He looks like a sixty-year-old truck driver, while she, I guess, is forty-five, a voluptuously plump, attractive woman who looks like a pleasant, happy homemaker. But I begin to suspect she is a prostitute.

As I watch them, the door on the truck to my right opens, and a man in his twenties exits the cab. He joins the couple, quickly taking over the conversation with the woman, and the older man fades back and returns to his truck. Both the young man and the woman smile as they talk. After a couple of minutes, they walk to his truck, and he opens the door. He helps her up the steps, follows her in, and closes the door. I see them kiss and fall back out of sight, presumably onto the bed as the truck slightly rocks, then stops. He appears without his shirt, and I see him putting up the privacy curtain that covers the truck's windows. Shortly, the truck starts gently rocking again but before long rocks lively, and I know they aren't dancing.

After about a half hour, the rocking stops, the curtain comes down, the door opens, and the woman climbs out aided by the young man. She smiles, he smiles, they exchange some pleasantries inaudible to me, and she turns and walks away between two trucks and disappears.

SMOKING

On a sunny evening, people head home from work, focused like moths to a light. They cut in and out of the heavy traffic, racing one another in the five lanes just to move ahead a car length or two. I occupy the third lane from the right and have a generous safety margin in front of me. Then, suddenly, two cars in the two right lanes, perhaps realizing those lanes exit, dive in front of me. Simultaneously, three cars on my left, obviously wanting to exit, do the same, and all five cars hit their brakes and stop.

"Damn!" Scanning my mirrors, I discover cars on both sides of my truck block any escape. I ram the brakes while steadying the steering wheel, and the brakes lock up. Looking to my mirrors, I see a dense cloud of black smoke belching from the eighteen tractor trailer tires as they burn on the pavement and leave black streaks that will remain there for months. In the next seconds, the tractor trailer begins jackknifing into the left lane, forcing me to ease off the brake. As I do, I rapidly bear down on the car in front of me.

Again braking, while watching the trailer in my mirrors, I try to stop my eighty-thousand-pound behemoth before it slams into the car. In a few, brief seconds the truck rushes forward, quickly closing the gap. The brakes grab and smoke, and ten feet from the car's plastic bumper, the truck stops. Scanning my mirrors, I laugh because now there aren't any cars anywhere near me.

ALWAYS TO WONDER

On a sunny Memorial Day weekend, I head east on I-440 in Nashville, and as the two eastbound lanes rise in a left-curving arch over I-24, the holiday traffic slows. Up ahead I see the right lane is blocked by an accident, and cars and trucks are merging left. At the bottleneck sits a sporty, red convertible, a tractor trailer, and a motorcycle spilled over onto the pavement. A young couple lingers near the motorcycle comforting each other, yet their appearance suggests they belong to the convertible. At the right rear of the tractor trailer stand, I guess, the truck's two drivers. Between the truck and the guardrail, lies someone mostly hidden by the truck's tires. Only the lower parts of two legs clad in men's jeans and the feet in tennis shoes are visible. He must be the motorcycle driver. How did he get back there, eighty feet from his motorcycle?

    The truck drivers do not attend to him, and I suppose that is because he is dead. I slowly pass by the body, the two truck drivers, the truck, the young couple, and finally the motorcycle, picking up speed to go on, never to know, yet always to wonder, what happened.

I can still see that scene: the young couple, the two truck drivers, and the legs of the motorcyclist. Only his life ended, but all our lives were affected—and who knows how many more.

YOUR TRUCK IS ON FIRE

The pelting rain has stopped, though blanketing clouds still block out the moon and stars. I look up at the dark mass as I monotonously breeze down the highway, wondering if it will rain again. As I do, a car overtakes me, its lights brightly glaring from my mirrors into my eyes. When alongside me, the car hangs there, matching my speed instead of passing. Surprised at this, I look down and see the passenger window open. A woman is frantically waving me over. Well, now what's the problem? Braking, I gradually slow the truck to a stop on the shoulder. The car stops in front of me. A door opens, and a young man hurries back to my truck.

"Your truck is on fire," he excitedly tells me.

"Where?"

"On the back," he says, pointing.

I check my mirror half expecting to see flames leaping into the night but only see impenetrable darkness. Something had alarmed the young man, though. Still, the only thing back there that could burn is a tire, and I would see intense flames feeding thick, black smoke up into the night sky. Yet, there is nothing.

"Oh, okay, thanks for stopping. I'll take care of it," I tell him, trying to sound appreciative. However, because of the late hour, my voice lacks urgency or concern, and I see confusion and disappointment on his face.

Hesitantly, he responds, echoing my own reply. "Oh, okay." Realizing there is nothing else to say or do, he reluctantly returns to his car. I watch it disappear into the night.

Checking the back of the trailer, I don't find a fire. Yet, on inspecting the tires, I find a flat with the steel core showing and know what happened. As I sped down the highway, the core scraped the pavement, causing a shower of sparks to shoot out in every direction. It must have looked like a half dozen sparklers on the Fourth of July, which anyone could mistake for a fire.

THE SHOW

An attractive blonde in her early thirties steps from a truck fueling on the truck stop's fuel island. She wears white shorts and a short-sleeved blouse and carries a small dog. Taking the dog to the grassy spot next to the island, she sets the leashed dog down on the grass. As he explores every inch, the curvaceous, young woman, with her back turned to a row of twenty trucks, swishes her shoulder-length hair, while slightly twisting her torso.

She intermittently continues this sensuous provocation for ten minutes until the dog entangles himself in the leash. Bending from the waist to free him tightens the shorts on her butt and gives a show to anyone looking. A driver leaving the fuel island spots her, for as he curves around the end of the island to leave, I see him craning his neck to get a better view. As he drives away, her dog finishes, and she gathers him in her arms, again briefly bending over before returning to the truck, and the show is over.

Think about this. She didn't do anything deliberate or wrong, but maybe she should have been more aware.

Drivers are cooped up in their trucks for days, weeks, even months at a time, away from their wives and girlfriends. Not long after this a driver's wife who got up in the middle of the night to go inside to the restroom, was found raped and murdered the nest morning, behind a dumpster.

BYE-BYE BABY

On a clear spring day, bunches of traffic, moving in waves, catch and engulf my truck, while steadily working to pass and pull away. In the current knot of cars and trucks, a small pickup has an open sliding window behind the driver's head. As it passes, the driver turns around to face me and gives me the finger, surprising me. He shakes his fist and fiercely yells—what, I don't know, for it doesn't penetrate the truck's engine noise. I suppose he curses me, yet I have no idea why. He does this twice, for ten or fifteen seconds each time, while driving seventy miles an hour and tailgating a car. I am so dumbfounded, I don't look away. If the car in front of him abruptly brakes, it's "Bye-bye, baby."

What an idiot! I have since been warned not to acknowledge, not even to look at, men like him, because it only incites them more. Somehow acknowledging them validates their behavior and gives them power and control, and that's what they want.

THE BALL AND THE BRAKE

A light drifting rain falls through cold air on Christmas in Portland, Oregon, and freezes onto buildings, parked cars, and trees, whose branches bend progressively downward with the weight. As I head across town to a fuel stop, the blacktop doesn't seem especially slick, but I cautiously drive as I continue down a side street. Ahead of me, the two-lane, one-way street crosses a bridge over the interstate highway. On approaching the bridge, I notice the concrete surface shines in the morning light, a sign of ice.

Warily, I begin crossing the span and immediately sense the ice through the lightness of the steering wheel and the subtle movements of my truck. This sensation so unnerves me, my muscles tense with an urge to brake. Yet I know better and instead roll free like a ball.

As I do, a fast-paced car overtakes me on my right. When the driver hits the ice, his brake lights flash, and he spins out of control in a sliding circle, headed toward me. "Please don't hit me," I say aloud as I carefully drift left. Because I turn the steering wheel so little, no one watching could tell I turned it at all. The car's rear end sweeps toward the side of my truck, and I brace for the impact. But he swishes by, missing my trailer by inches, as I keep straight and easy, free rolling over the bridge. The car continues to spin until smacking into the concrete guardrail with a jarring *crunch*.

LOOK AT THESE POOR FOOLS DRIVING IN THIS RAINSTORM IN THE DARK

On a Sunday night, I drive north on I-75 from Dayton, Ohio, through a construction zone with two northbound lanes. A concrete divider edges the left lane, and the right lane is without a shoulder, making both lanes narrow and tight. Heavy traffic, mostly cars, surrounds my truck.

Now the rain begins, lightly at first, just sparse droplets on the glass. Then a sudden downpour drenches the windshield. With the deluge, brake lights flash and surprised drivers swerve in the narrow lanes, threatening to involve all of us in an accident. The pounding rain floods the road, the divider catching the sudden flow and turning the roadway into a stream. The truck's tires cut the water and throw it airborne in a wave that drowns the windshields of nearby cars.

Straining to see through my flooded windshield, hemmed in by half-blinded drivers on my right, I tensely plow through the water inches from the concrete divider. When lightning flashes, I abstractly think someone with a giant camera snapped a picture and perhaps remarked, "Look at these poor fools driving in this rainstorm in the dark."

WHEN BIRDS

In Illinois, freshly harvested fields edged by scattered trees stretch from the highway as I pass by. The spring and summer, now played out, give way to flocks of birds that climb, dive, and swirl, breaking apart and rushing together in acrobatic flight. These birds foretell the fast approaching fall, days of drenching rain, and days of brilliant angled light shining through golden falling leaves.

ANGEL

"You are at the wrong place," a man tells me.

That isn't what I want to hear after a long, tiring day as I stand in a warehouse at ten o'clock at night expecting to pick up a load.

"You have to go to our other warehouse. Here is what you do," he says, giving me directions.

Unfortunately, what he tells me—to turn left out of the driveway where, three blocks ahead, I will see a light—isn't what I hear, or it's not what I remember hearing once I return to my truck. Let me see now, he said to turn left out of the yard and, at the first right, turn right. Yet, when I look down the street and see a light, I remember, "At the first light, turn right and take the first left onto Fourteenth Avenue. The warehouse is on the left."

Therefore, at the light I turn right one block to the first left, Fourteenth Avenue, stop, and look left up Fourteenth. I see a wooded, hilly residential neighborhood and think, *Oh no, this does not look right.* Still, I reason this is the right street, because sometimes residential subdivisions border industrial parks. I don't like the looks of this one bit, though. However, because I am tired, and part of my brain is already asleep, I turn. Heavy old trees line the street, and behind them, heavy old houses, trim and orderly, sit perched on banks with steps leading down from them. On seeing this, a nagging doubt that I have messed up ties my gut into a knot. The road winds farther up the hill until bending left and heading down two blocks to a T, and it is then I know I am lost. Damn, now what do I do?

I am inclined to turn left, returning the direction I came. As I turn, however, I discover I cannot round the corner because of a parked car in front of an old, two-story house set high and back from the street. Though now eleven o'clock at night, light floods the house without a single dark pane of glass, my first piece of luck.

Going up the sidewalk, I cross the lawn and climb the steps to the porch. Large windows with open curtains bracket a front door with an oval, beveled-glass window. Peering into the house, I don't see anyone. So I knock firmly but not too loudly, hoping someone will hear but won't be frightened. No one comes. I knock again, slightly louder, and a woman, who must have been on her way, quickly appears. She is slim, in her late forties, and has short-cropped hair tinged with gray. She wears a wispy nightgown a slight wind could lift and whisk away into the night. What's more, she looks frightened. She stops five feet from the door and doesn't come closer. I have to talk through the glass, pitching my voice strongly forward in hopes of her hearing and understanding me.

"Hi, I am a truck driver, and I am lost. You can see my truck there in the street," I say, motioning with my hand to where my truck sits with its lights on. "I cannot turn the corner and was wondering—if that is your car there, are you willing to move it?" She looks out at my truck and again at me. Responding inaudibly through the glass, she turns and disappears through a doorway. My heart sinks. I just stand there, stupidly, I suppose, not knowing what to do, but before I can react, she returns, dressed, and opens the door without hesitation.

"Where do you want to go?" she asks in a soft voice, which I realize is why her words never penetrated the glass. When I tell her, she says, "Oh, I know where that is, but you won't be able to get out of here by yourself. Follow my car, and I will take you there."

"That's nice of you. Thank you," I say, sincerely grateful.

After pulling away from the curb, she drives a short distance and stops, waiting for me. I carefully and successfully negotiate the turn, managing to stay off the grass and not hit any signs or poles. She starts down the street, and I follow to a stop sign where she turns right. After a block and a half, we approach a construction zone, and I wince. The street is a mess, torn to pieces with an open ditch on both sides of a narrow, winding traffic lane lined by a hodgepodge of orange cones, barricades, and barrels. *How will I ever get through that?*

She continues, and I cautiously follow, managing to keep my nervousness in check. Slowly I move forward through the maze, ever watchful of the ditches beside me, sharply aware I could easily drop tires off the edge and slam the axle down onto the asphalt. Thankfully, there aren't any sharp bends. My truck stiffly weaves through the orange jungle, only nudging two cones. Whew!

Driving on, we come to another T, and this time she turns left, and I follow until she stops, her red taillights flashing in the dark. We are at the street I turned from into the residential area. She turns right to the light and then left up the street I first came down. A block farther and she turns left onto the street, where I should have turned right and saved myself this grief. One block more and we are at Fourteenth Street and turning left. There, two hundred feet on the left, I see the warehouse. She makes a U-turn and, as she passes to return home, points at the building. I wave and mouth, "Thank you," and she smiles as she drives away, my angel in the night.

What can I say? I got myself into this mess. Yet that's not what's of consequence in this story. A woman alone in her nightgown in the middle of the night took it upon herself to help me. She had to have been frightened at first.

CROSSOVER CONSEQUENCE

A Wyoming snowstorm pummels the truck, and as I drive through the night, the wipers only partly shove away the snow. The build-up freezes onto the blades, causing them to ride up and leave wide blurry streaks that partially obscure my vision. Straining to see in the dark, I anxiously push ahead, worried that if I stop to clear away the snow and ice, I will be stuck. Gradually, though, the blurry mess obscures my vision to the point where I cannot go on.

Cautiously, I pull onto the shoulder, pressing through the snow and slowing to a stop. Afraid another truck might hit me, I turn on my flashers before rolling down the window to reach out and around, grab hold of the wiper, and bang the blade against the glass. The ice shatters off as the cold chills me, and snow blows into the cab. When I finish, the wiper sweeps a clear half circle in front of me. *Well, that's better. Now I hope I can get out of here.*

With nervous anticipation, I shift into low, slowly releasing the clutch until the gear engages. With relief, I feel the tires take hold, and the truck begins steadily moving out onto the highway. Snow, shining in the headlights' beams, swirls and blows over and around me, steadily building on the roadway. As my speed increases, the road's slick surface skims under my tires. The truck feels light, and the steering wheel is loose enough to twirl with my little finger.

With a steady, gentle touch, I push forward through the storm. Scanning ahead across the median, I notice another tractor trailer in the eastbound lanes, and as I watch, it begins jackknifing. *Uh-oh, what's happening there?* It straightens but then dives into the median plowing through the snow. Before I can react, it emerges onto the westbound lanes a short ways in front of me. *Shit!* It eases to an angled broadside stop with its nose on the right shoulder and blocking both lanes. *Damn! I cannot stop. No way. He's too close.* I have mere seconds before I smash into him.

The left shoulder is open, though the rear of the truck's trailer is flush with the edge of the lane, leaving only the narrow shoulder to squeeze through. With quick decision, I move left. If I bear too far left, I will drop the left wheels off the pavement and likely roll over, slamming the driver's side of the truck into the ground. Too far right, I will shear off my right-hand mirrors or, worse, ram the end of the trailer with the right side of my truck.

In a breathless rush, I am there, watching the shoulder edge on the left, watching the mirrors on the right, and *whoosh* I fly by the end of the trailer and push on through the storm.

Whoa! Can you believe this? I figured I would at least knock off my mirrors. I got lucky again.

I'M NOT SUPPOSED TO DO THIS, SHE SAYS

Having waited four hours at a Salt Lake City, Utah, warehouse to pick up a load of recyclable paper, the trailer is finally loaded, and I am ready to leave. On engaging the clutch, the trailer resists, the truck's diesel engine hunkering down as the trailer sluggishly creeps forward up the sloped driveway to the dock. This surprises and worries me, and I wonder how the weight sits distributed on the axles.

Once clear of the dock, I get out and, closing the doors, I look inside the trailer. I see ragged, five-foot square, double-stacked bundles of newspapers, magazines, and computer paper. The bundles, stacked close to the ceiling and sides, reach within a foot of the end. Seeing this, I frown, knowing from experience too much weight sits on the rear axles.

Driving to a nearby truck stop with a CAT scale, I weigh and discover the rear axles carry two thousand pounds over the limit. *Wow, this is bad.* Adjusting the axles will not correct the overage. I must return to the shipper. Once there, I wait three more hours for a dock and fifteen minutes for the shipper to adjust the load. Afterward, the forklift driver tells me I am ready to go.

"What did you do?" I ask.

"Moved some of the weight. It should be okay now."

"Okay," I reluctantly agree, and he returns inside. I hoped he would remove some weight, but shippers resist that because they ship less for the same cost. Unfortunately, when they don't load the trailer correctly the first time, they usually don't get it right the second time either. Returning to the scale, I find the rear axles still carry a thousand pounds over the limit. Annoyed and frustrated, I return to the shipper. Handing the scale ticket to the scowling clerk, I say, "The trailer is still too heavy."

"We ship them that way all the time," he sharply shoots back. "Are you sure you have your axles adjusted correctly?"

"Yes, I have adjusted them all that I can. It won't work," I state firmly.

Gruffly he replies, "There is an open dock, back it in there."

"I already have," I tell him. He brushes by me, leaving the office. I see him speaking to the forklift driver as I leave the warehouse and return to my truck. Sitting in the cab, I twice hear the forklift enter and leave the trailer, and soon a man stands at my window.

"Give me your bills," he gruffly directs me, and I hand them to him. He makes changes before handing them back to me without a word, walking away from the truck and returning inside.

Looking at the bills, I see they removed two bundles. I am relieved, for certainly, now I have legal axle weights. The truck stop scale confirms this, and I am finally ready to go. By now the sun hangs low in the sky. This concerns me, because although the first sixty miles of my trip follow I-15, I must drive Highway 6, the narrow, winding, two-lane road through Price River Canyon, in the dark. I am not happy about that.

I start out and, an hour later, reach Spanish Fork, Utah and exit onto Highway 6. The first few miles pass through strip malls and homes, which gradually give way to Price River Canyon. Once in the canyon, the highway bends and twists, following the river. At times the river spreads and thins to a mere creek edged by towering cottonwood trees and grassy pastures that at night attract foraging deer.

As I curve along the narrow highway, I am alone and seldom meet an approaching car. My headlights faintly reach into the moonless night when, suddenly in a flashing movement from my right, three deer bound in front of the truck. They block the width of the highway, leaving no way around them. *Uh-oh!* Braking hard, I hold the truck straight and steady to avoid a jackknife. The truck's tires burn on the blacktop as, *thump*, I clip one deer. In another instant, all three disappear into the dark as I keep going, never stopping, building my speed into the night.

Five miles farther on, I reach an open Utah weigh station. As I drive onto the scale, the attendant checks the weights on her monitor, her calm, expressionless face easily visible. A second later, her eyes abruptly widen, and she reaches for the button that changes the scale light from green to red. Immediately I stop, a sinking feeling rushing through my body. *Oh no, what has happened?*

The officer leaves the building and approaches my truck. I roll down the window to hear her say, "You are four thousand pounds over on your drive axles. Pull up to the side, park, and come inside with all your paperwork."

With my heart in my stomach, I do as I'm told, aware four thousand pounds will incur a whopper fine. Taking the necessary paperwork, I go to the office. The DOT officer prepares a ticket as I quietly wait. Soon she looks up and repeats what she said outside, her solemnity affirming the seriousness of the violation.

"You are four thousand pounds over on your drives," she says. "I need your CDL and truck registration."

As she repeats the offense, I know hammering the brakes to avoid the deer jammed the paper bundles into the nose of the trailer. Therefore, as I hand over the documents, I mount a defense, saying, "I have three CAT scale tickets showing I made every possible attempt to scale the load, returning twice to the shipper. It took nearly eight hours to finish loading. About five miles from here, I had to brake hard to avoid three deer on the road. The load must have slid forward," I tell her.

The officer looks at me with sympathy and replies, "I have to give you an overweight ticket. Also, if I open the trailer and see the load has shifted, I will have to give you a ticket for failing to secure the load properly. I think it would be best if I don't open the trailer. Can you move your tandems to correct your weight?" she asks.

"I can correct some of it," I tell her.

"Pull around back and move your axles and then pull back onto the scale."

Behind the scale house, I inspect the trailer's tandem axles, counting eight holes I can use, which should shift about twenty-five hundred pounds, leaving about a fifteen-hundred-pound violation. After moving the axles, I return to the scale and watch the officer studying the readout. She waves me on to park, and then I return to the office.

"Sign here," she says, pointing to a line on the completed ticket.

Signing, I see the fine is over one hundred dollars. As she separates the copies, I moan, "Now what am I going to do? I still have another scale farther on I have to cross."

Looking at me compassionately, she says, "Wait a minute." I watch as she dials a phone number while saying, "I'm not supposed to do this." After a dozen unanswered rings, she tells me, "That scale is closed."

"Thank you," I say sincerely. "Am I all right to go now?"

"Yes, you are."

Another of my angels.

KIRK IS A CURIOUS KID

As I awake in the morning at a friend's house at Tucson, Arizona, sunlight streams into the room. When I turn in bed to see a clock, the face reads 7:45, not too early to rise, for I hear my friend busy in the kitchen. Once dressed, I go to join her.

"Would you like hot chocolate?" she asks me.

"Yes, I would," I readily agree.

"Kirk said good morning to you," she tells me, knowing I did not hear him. Kirk is her twelve-year-old grandson. I look around for a moment before I see him bundled in a blanket on the couch.

Stepping into the living room, which is open to the kitchen, I tell him, "Good morning. I didn't hear you, what with these hearing aids, which don't always work for me. How did you sleep last night?"

"Good," he answers.

"I suppose I have you to thank for hot chocolate. You are having hot chocolate, right?" I ask him.

"Yes, I am."

"Hot chocolate is great. I used to have it sometimes when I was a kid," I tell him. My friend brings in two steaming mugs, which Kirk and I take into the kitchen. We sit at the kitchen table opposite each other, each of us holding our mug between our two hands while appreciating the heat warming our fingers and palms.

Kirk sips his chocolate and says, "It tastes like marshmallows."

"It tastes creamy," I say.

He stirs his chocolate and removes the spoon, holding it sideways over the cup, the concave dip of the spoon toward me. He watches the steam rising off the metal spoon and disappearing into the air. With the steam trailing away, he again dips the spoon into the chocolate, stirring the dark mixture three or four times before removing the spoon and holding it over his cup like before. Again, he watches the steam rising and disappearing, and I approvingly think, *Kirk is a curious kid.*

MAN HAS SEEN THE PICTURES

At the Clark Truck Stop at Plainfield, Illinois, a suburb of Chicago, three or four inches of snow cover the ground with more snow falling and blowing in a cold, biting wind, well below thirty degrees. With the engine running, I have the heater turned on high, the fan full blast. Yet I shiver, for the beating wind forces cold air into the cab from around the doors. I think if I go into the truck stop for a while, perhaps the truck will warm up when I'm gone. Anyway, I would like to buy milk for cereal I prepare on a hot plate and, at least, warm myself that way.

Bundled in a sock cap, gloves, and down jacket, I open the door. As I climb out, the wind shoves the door hard against me. I force it back, stepping into the snow and turning while closing the door behind me. Leaning against the wind, I push forward, and stinging pellets of snow blur my vision. Head down, I glance up occasionally to avoid bumping into trailers. My feet crunch in the snow as I weave between tractor trailers. As I pass each truck, I hear the engine's deep growl and wonder if the driver is staying warm.

In front of the convenience store, I stomp as much snow as I can off my feet before entering the store. Once inside, I relax and wander around, looking at the too-familiar choices—crackers, chips, and candy—and finally head to the cooler. I only manage a few steps when a man blocks my path and speaks to me, seemingly unaware of his rudeness. I don't understand the first sentences but hear, "My wife left me. She ran off with the guy next door." My antagonist, for that's what I consider him, looks thirty-five or so, and six foot tall. He has long brown hair and thick eyeglasses and wears ordinary work clothes.

As I appraise him, he continues to talk. "After she left, I didn't get angry or anything. I just didn't know what to do. So I just thought about it and said, 'What the heck, I will write some women in prison.' Someone told me about that. I thought I would just be honest and tell them I am fixed. Most of these women are in their thirties and probably still want to have children, so I didn't think any would respond, but guess what? I wrote thirty-five letters and got answers from almost all of them."

I wonder if he sent each woman the same letter. I suppose he probably did. I believe I would have. He produces several pictures of attractive women from his pocket and fans them like a deck of cards.

"This one," he says, pointing to a smiling blonde, "has written me several times, but I don't know what it would cost to get her out on parole and all."

I don't understand what cost he refers to but don't ask.

He continues, "Her father abused her as a child, and her first husband beat her. She almost constantly had bruises somewhere on her body," he says. "Her second husband forced her to commit armed robbery, and that's why she is in prison."

These images, one after the other, rush at me like stampeding horses, causing me to want to stop them. Thus, I gesture by holding up my hand, palm toward him, and say, "Enough!"

Looking at me with a hurt expression, he says, "Okay."

Stepping past him, I continue to the cooler for milk, which I pay for at the front counter. As I open the door to leave the store, I see my friend, again smiling, has cornered a man in his late twenties who politely listens. As I push open the door and step into the frigid air, I wonder if he has seen the pictures yet.

FRIGHTENED AT FLAGSTAFF

As I approach Flagstaff, Arizona, from the west, I-40 climbs out of the high desert's sagebrush plateau and into the evergreens and aspens of the San Francisco Mountains. Six inches of snow cover the ground, and packed snow and ice encase the roadway, causing traffic to slow to a crawl. In the median sit several abandoned cars and a tractor trailer sprawled over on its side with boxes spilling out of the trailer. Four cars ahead of me creep at twenty-five miles an hour as lazily drifting snowflakes fall through the dark night.

Past Flagstaff, the snow stops, the road clears, and the cars pull away. Bare black asphalt stretches out before me, and I speed up to fifty-five miles an hour. Yet I notice the asphalt shines in the headlights' beams, and I think *black ice.* On Realizing that, my apprehension ratchets up a notch. I feel the ice through the steering wheel, and know Ice needs a steady but delicate touch, no fancy moves, and absolutely no braking.

As the truck flies down the highway, the steering wheel feels loose and light, as though the wheels are barely touching the road, and I know I cannot stop and shouldn't try. Up ahead, I notice a car's brake lights flash and disappear, and wonder, *What's happening there?*

Farther on I spot a car beside the road, probably the one I saw from a ways back. The front wheels rest on the shoulder, and the rear wheels sit buried in snow, sloping down into the median, the headlights angled into the sky. Approaching closer, I see six Asian women inside, five older passengers and a twenty-something driver. They sit unmoving, not talking, just staring straight ahead, the driver stiffly clutching the steering wheel. They look petrified, their faces transfixed with fright.

My mind rolls time back, and I imagine the young woman as she drives on the ice, the slippery, unnerving feeling. She panics and hits the brake pedal. The brakes lock, the car slides, and the frightened driver oversteers, sending the car into a terrifying spin. The women scream. The car slides out of control, and flying off the road, abruptly stops in the snow on the shoulder.

Did I stop to help them? No, I didn't. I would have had to stop on the highway, for I couldn't get onto the shoulder. Doing this would create an additional hazard. Another driver might come along and, seeing the semi and the car, hit the brakes and perhaps smash into the women. Someone else would come along to help them.

A HURRICANE WILL SOON HIT THE FLORIDA PANHANDLE

From the radio, I hear warnings of a hurricane racing north along the west coast of Florida, which authorities expect to cross the Florida Panhandle soon. As I travel east on I-10, this worries me, because this storm and I follow a collision course. Even now, rain and a brisk wind rock the trailer, prompting me to find somewhere to park. Luckily, ahead I see a TA Travel Plaza and, on exiting the interstate, discover the plaza only a third full. Two trucks parked parallel to the building block the windows from the expectant gale force of the hurricane. The rest of the trucks sit parked in a single row and, pulling alongside them, I shut down to await the storm.

The rain is letting up, but I think this is a brief lull, so I decide to go inside for dinner before it starts again. As I walk across the parking lot, the rain begins, and I burst forth in a run, exhilarated in the wind and rain as I race across the lot. On entering the building, I find a shadowy half-light, and my mood drops as I realize the power is off, and the store is closed. Disappointed, I return to the truck, hurrying back through the rain.

Before long the storm's tempo intensifies as the wind bangs and pushes the tractor trailer in a rough, rocking motion. The pounding force of the storm echoes inside the cab, engulfing me. As I quietly sit in the driver's seat, a sheet of water drowns the windshield. Through the side window, I see a deluge of water, pushed by the wind, overwhelm the drainage and flood the blacktopped lot. The onslaught perseveres as dusk deepens into a moonless night. Feeling sleepy, I pull away from the storm into myself. Retiring to bed, I lie there not expecting to sleep, but in a few minutes, I do just that.

When I wake up, the truck sits motionless in dark quiet. In the stillness I am reluctant to move, thinking the storm may resume at any second. Yet it doesn't, and I drift off to sleep again. In the morning, the truck stop's windows stand intact, the building undamaged, with just a few leaves and small branches scattered about the lot.

JOLLY ROGER

Having scaled my truck at the Denver, Colorado, Flying J Truck Stop, I park to go inside for the scale ticket and a gallon of water. As I climb out of the cab, a young man in his mid-twenties approaches me.

"Driver would you like your wheels polished?" he asks.

I couldn't care less whether I have shiny wheels. Still, I like to help others who want to work instead of just begging, so I say, "How much do you charge?" knowing wheel polishers charge five dollars for each wheel.

"Five dollars a wheel," he says.

I agree, because the work will only cost me ten dollars as only the two steer tires have aluminum wheels.

"Oh, thank you, driver," he says with obvious relief. "I haven't had a job in three days. I was doing well over at the TA, but they started charging a ten-dollar parking fee, and that chased off the owner-operators, who are my best customers. They chased us out, too," he says, with "us" likely the various people hustling drivers for money.

"Your wheels are pretty scratched up," he advises me as he looks at the driver's side wheel.

"Wait until you see the other one," I tell him. "That wheel has a groove in it. I don't care, though. I only have them polished, because I feel sorry for the guys trying to make a living doing this." Immediately, I regret saying this, for no one wants pity. I think I've offended him, but he deflects the remark.

"Don't feel too sorry for them," he says. "They are all a bunch of crackheads." To prove he isn't one of them, he tells me, "I was a truck driver. See, I still have my CDL and my company ID." He removes them from his wallet to show me. "Besides, I have a motor home to keep running. It's how I live."

The key sentence here, of course, is, "I was a truck driver."

"I was making $48,000 a year, and I still remember my truck and ID numbers," he says proudly.

Now I am curious. "What happened?"

"I got a DUI," he says, rather unhappily.

Whoa, bad news, I think. A DUI is bad for anyone, but for a truck driver, a DUI simply blows a hole in your life.

"My grandmother had a heart attack and died, and I just went nuts. I went on a binge. I left my truck at my house and drove to my grandmother's house in Tennessee. I don't remember much about it except waking up in jail and thinking, *Oh shit, what have I done?* My grandmother was like my mother. She was my mother. She raised me."

"Were you in an accident?" I ask apprehensively.

"No, no, nothing like that, just wasted out of my mind and, I guess, not driving very well, and so I got stopped."

I don't say but think, *Lucky you. An accident with a DUI would have been much worse.* Yet I don't understand how he still has his CDL. I guess he would have lost his license. No matter, though, because no trucking company will hire him, or at least, so I believe.

"I am going to get it back," he says. I am confused about what he means but believe he refers to his job and life before the DUI.

"I will probably have to go back to an in-house school (a truck-driving school taught by the company you will eventually work for)."

"What about your old employer?" I offer. "Could you go back with them?"

"No, they won't take me back," he says, while diligently polishing the first wheel. "They say I abandoned my truck, even though I left it parked in front of my house."

"You are still a young man," I say. "You have time to work it out, and you have the determination to do so."

"Yeah, I am going to get a driving job again, and then I am going to get my own truck," he says with a smile.

I don't understand if he is on probation or the steps necessary for him to return to driving, but I don't ask, because sometimes there are just too many questions.

"When I get my own truck, I am going to have a crossbones and Jolly Roger painted on the side of it," he enthusiastically proclaims.

Not knowing how to respond, I just smile, hoping that will show my appreciation. As I watch, he finishes the first wheel and moves around to the passenger-side wheel. Meanwhile I retreat to my cab. When he comes back around to my side, I roll down the window.

"I was able to get most of the paint out of that groove in your wheel," he says.

"Thanks," I tell him. I owe him ten dollars, but I want to give him twenty. Yet how can I do it without bruising his ego? I fold a twenty and hand the bill down to where he stands below my window. As I give it to him, I say with firm conviction, "This looks like a twenty, but it is actually a ten." He flushes, making me wonder if I have done the right thing.

"Thank you, driver," he says. "My CB handle is Bones. If you see my truck someday, give me a buzz."

I don't have a CB and don't mention it, but instead reply, "Good luck to you! I will watch for your truck."

He walks off between two trailers, perhaps looking for another job. Fifteen minutes later, as I leave the truck stop, an old motor home comes up behind me and passes, and I recognize my wheel polisher when I see him wave. I am half-surprised not to see crossbones and Jolly Roger painted on the side of it, but after all, this is a temporary arrangement for him, don't you think?

I love these stories about people "out of the loop" that I met on my travels.

IT JUST MAKES ME WONDER

It is dark when I arrive at the Tomahawk Truck Stop at Brush, Colorado, northeast of Denver. Water-filled potholes and endless mud from a recent storm make up the parking lot. From experience I know water-filled holes look harmless; however, if they are deep, a wheel could drop to the axle, leaving the truck hopelessly stuck. So I avoid as many of them as possible. Still, my truck jumps into and out of one hole after another, jostling me up and down, tossing objects from shelves and the upper bunk onto the floor. Finally I manage to push back into a space and stop. Picking up DVDs, coats, books, and exercise equipment, I put them away before undressing and settling down for the night.

In the morning, I decide to return an audiobook to the convenience store and look for a new one to rent. I approach the store concentrating on keeping mud off my shoes. Only when I reach it do I see a handsome, muscular young man, possibly in his twenties, standing near the door. Though it's a cold morning, he wears jeans and a sleeveless T-shirt slit down under the arm, exposing many half-inch cuts lacing his bare skin. He appears dazed, and I wonder if he has been fighting or if he is on drugs. As I pass him, he doesn't hit on me for money, and this surprises me, because he looks as though he expects something. Maybe he's waiting for someone to pick him up. Anyway, I go inside and exchange the audiobook for a different one.

When I come out, he is gone. Returning to my truck, I start out, pulling into the street where, to my surprise, the young man stands on the shoulder. But he isn't thumbing. He just stands there with his head bent, looking confused and rocking back and forth on his feet, and I wonder how someone so young can be so fucked-up.

BIG AND SWEET

At 2:00 a.m., I awake to my loud, annoying alarm. Reaching out into the chilly air, I silence the noisy pest. Afterward, pulling the four blankets piled on me snug to my sides, I lie quietly still in the dark, procrastinating and protesting. *It's too cold to get up.* Yet I have to.

Finally I climb out of bed to turn on the ignition and hear the diesel engine chug over, catch, and growl, filling the cab with a familiar hum. Once dressed, I pull on my coat and cap, exit the cab, and walk to the convenience store. When I drive this early, I need something to eat. Overhead, a bright moon and countless stars fill the New Mexico night sky, and the crisp air sharpens my senses. Once inside the store, I amble about two short aisles—all this independent truck stop has to offer—and think, *Darn, they don't have much here to eat.*

I settle on a bag of taco chips I can munch on while driving and an ice-cream bar, a square chunk of vanilla coated with chocolate. *That should give me an energy bump*, I think. When I reach the counter, a tall, heavy young woman with plain features smiles down at me from the raised floor behind the counter. With her straight, straw-blond hair tied back behind her head, she looks ordinary, except for her disarming smile. She reminds me of voluptuous women I've seen in museum paintings. Swaying slightly from side to side, perhaps to a song playing in her head, she intrigues me as she rings up my chips and ice cream, and I think, *What a charmer.*

"Eating ice cream on a cold night?" she says to me in a smooth, questioning tone.

"When you like ice cream like I do, you can eat it anytime," I assert.

"You know what I would like right now?" she says, "A big bucket of Häagen Dazs."

I smile up at her, thinking, *Yeah, big and sweet, just like you.*

MORNING STAR

I have a Rival two-quart slow cooker, with one temperature setting, in my truck that I use to bake apples. It holds two medium-sized apples.

To prepare baked apples, use wax-free apples if available, and do not peel them. I like to use Yellow Delicious. Core the apples out from the top, leaving the bottom intact, which you can remove once the apples cook. Sprinkle powdered cinnamon into the cavity to coat it, and fill the cavity two-thirds with raisins, pressing them down with the tip of a finger. Top those with chopped walnuts, also pressing them down until the apple is full. Do not add sugar, for it overpowers the apple flavor, and it's unnecessary, because apples and raisins contain natural sugar. Place the apples in the cooker, shaving them slightly on the sides if they do not fit.

The time needed to cook the apples varies with the hardness of the apple. Soft apples take a shorter time to cook; hard apples take longer. Cook with the lid on, and check in about an hour. When the skins split, the apples are done. Try different apples to find your favorite. To serve, put a single apple in a cereal bowl, and cut the apple from the top into four quarters. The sections will open like a star with the raisins and walnuts in the center. To finish, add milk or, if you prefer, a scoop of vanilla ice cream.

I didn't cook much, just mostly ate in truck stops. I wasn't going to include this, but these baked apples are great. Anyone can fix them, even someone who's usually a total zero in the kitchen. So try this, maybe even teach your kids, but supervise the knife.

SHE CALLS ME DADDY

Approaching the gate after completing loading at a customer, I'm ready to head out. As I stop, a man steps out of the guard shack. Seeing him, I roll down the window.

"I need your bills," he says.

I hand them to him, and he goes to the rear of the trailer to check the seal. I follow him back. That done, he asks for my driver's license number, state, and expiration date. When I tell him, he appraises me with a quick look and says, "You're about ready to retire. You don't look that old."

"I'm sixty," I flatly respond, not wanting to be sixty. Still I am pleased he thinks I look younger, though, of course, that doesn't make me younger.

He continues, "I'm thirty-eight and feel like sixty sometimes. I'm a diabetic."

"That is hard on you," I comment, glancing at his wiry, salt-and-pepper hair.

"Tell me about it," he gravely intones in the spirit of "Woe is me, I suffer and the world owes me homage."

Well, we all like sympathy sometimes, I think.

"I can't wait to finish my shift," he says. "I get three days off, and I am going to see my girl."

Immediately I assume he is divorced and has a little girl he pays child support for, an all-too-common affair these days. So I say, "You have a little girl?"

"No, she's my girl, though she calls me Daddy, and I haven't even touched her yet," he says with confident anticipation. "She lives in Memphis, and I am going to see her. She was my roommate's girlfriend, but they broke up. After a while, she and I started calling and using the Internet.

She isn't very pretty and somewhat fat, but she has large ga-wahs."

He, of course, means breasts, or at least I guess that's what he means.

"Pretty girls are all sweet and nice, but the next thing you know they are fucking around," he tells me. His expression suggests he knows from experience, or perhaps pretty girls reject him, and so he resents them.

Anyway, I think but don't say, *You don't have to be pretty to fuck around.* Instead I tell him, "Well, I hope you have a nice time in Memphis."

"Oh, I will," he assures me, stepping back from the truck with a smirk.

Engaging the transmission, I pull through the gate into the street as his words, "She calls me Daddy," resonate in my head like a mesmerizing lyric from a song.

A DARK RAIN

The evening traffic snarls around me in bunched masses as rain, dark in the night, splatters against the windshield. As I slow to exit the freeway down a sloping ramp, dozens of water drops attach themselves to the windows and mirrors, obstructing my sight. The windshield wipers swish back and forth, pushing that water off to the side, yet three or four greasy smudges smear with each swing the wipers make.

These streaks catch light that glares annoyingly in front of me as I turn right off the ramp.

With urgency I go a block and turn left into the Pilot Truck Stop. For, at this hour, the available spaces fill quickly, and I worry I cannot park. I cannot go elsewhere, because I am out of hours, so I must park here.

I scan for openings, and I see two, but I'm heading the wrong way. Looping around for an easier approach, I am stopped by a backing truck. I nervously wait several minutes as he slowly jacks around his tractor until finally rolling back and out of my way. Anxiously I return to the two spaces I first saw. To my relief, they haven't been filled. As I pass them, however, I realize they won't work because of the short turning radius fronting them.

Driving on, I spot another space, but I must do a U-turn between two rows of parked trucks, a risky maneuver on a dark, rainy night. If I leave to turn around, another truck could take the space. I decide to chance it. Cautiously I jackknife the trailer in the dark while blinded by the truck's curving angle. Pressing into the tightest horseshoe possible, the cab comes close to hitting the trailer. Meanwhile, the iron framing on the rear of the trailer swings in front of a half dozen fiberglass truck noses, easily crushed. Yet I cannot see them. I am a man with one blind eye in the dark and the rain.

As I cautiously loop through the curve, I nervously listen and feel for any noises or sudden lurches, the trailer hitting another truck. To my relief, I smoothly pull through without incident. At last straightening, I look for the opening and, seeing it, push back into the space. Once stopped, I turn off the wipers. As they slap one last time, I shut off the engine and the lights. In the dark, now I am ok as I quietly sit looking out at the rain.

WHAT DO HORSES KNOW OF LOVE?

Two horses standing side by side, head to flank, in a wide-open Texas prairie pasture, affectionately nuzzle and clean each other on a sunny day in May. As I pass by, I wonder, *What do horses know of love?*

RIGHT SIDED

It's a sunny Florida day on I-75, and the heavy traffic pushes at seventy-plus miles an hour. A ways in front of me a car rapidly overtakes a tractor trailer that is overtaking a slower car. As I watch, the tractor trailer moves to the left and begins passing. Meanwhile, the fast car catches up and, pulling onto the shoulder, passes the slower car on the right. The shoulder is barely wide enough for the fast car to slip by. The tractor trailer completes its pass, signals, and begins moving into the right lane in front of the slow car. At the same time, the fast car pulls into the right lane from the shoulder, and I know the tractor trailer cannot see it. They come close together until the tractor trailer jerks left to avoid hitting the fast car, and in my mind, I hear the driver exclaim, "Where in the hell did he come from?" The fast car takes the lane as the tractor trailer returns to the left lane, and the traffic keeps rolling on, heavy and pushing at seventy-plus miles an hour.

I saw this happen a couple of times in Florida, though nowhere else in the country, just Florida.

ANGRY, YOUNG MEN

On I-17 in Phoenix, Arizona, at 11:00 p.m. in light traffic, I look to my right mirror and see a pickup back a ways in the right lane. Signaling, I move into the right lane to exit onto I-10 west, which intersects a mile farther on. I give the pickup plenty of room, but because I am tired, I don't realize how fast it's approaching. Quickly catching up and whipping around me, the pickup cuts in front of me and speeds away. As it does, a young man leans out the passenger window and, turning back toward me, yells something and shakes his fist. When he does, I think, *Angry, young men shake their fists at the world.*

STUPID TRUCK DRIVER

With cruise control on, I run a steady pace not subject to the variations of my foot. On a smooth, level highway, the cruise works well. When I catch another vehicle, I know I am driving faster than they are and, once by, will pull away. Just now I rapidly catch a "slow-go," a car driving well below normal traffic speed. Scanning my mirrors, I see a car, but a ways back, so I signal and move into the left lane. I immediately realize I misjudged the speed of the oncoming car, because it quickly catches me, tailgating me. Holding my speed with the cruise, I pass the slow-go, signal, and move back into the right lane, rapidly pulling away.

The car, a Mercedes, passes, cuts in front of me, and immediately slows to thirty miles an hour, forcing me to brake. *Whoa, what is he doing?* Slowing, I glance into my mirrors, worried, because a car or truck could rear-end my trailer. Of course the Mercedes would speed away, leaving me with an accident. With the left lane clear, I change lanes, but the Mercedes, expecting this, swerves in front of me, again blocking me. "Damn!" In my mirrors, several other cars bear down so I swerve right, and the Mercedes moves with me, continuing to block me. There is no way I can pass him. He has me, and he knows it.

Meanwhile, the other cars reach us, and the Mercedes allows them to pass. I don't again try to pass. He holds me to thirty miles an hour for four or five miles as I anxiously watch my mirrors. I hope my flashers will alert approaching drivers soon enough to avoid rear-ending the trailer. Abruptly the Mercedes exits up a ramp to the stop, turns right, and disappears. As he does, in my mind I hear him saying, "I will teach you not to pull in front of me and slow me down, you stupid truck driver."

BEYOND THE WALL

Traveling a two-lane Iowa country road at night, I see my turn ahead, a road picked out on a map as the most direct route to my shipper. As I complete the turn, my headlights light up a sign, Low underpass, twelve feet six inches, a foot too low for the truck. My heart sinks. Now what do I do? Just past the sign, I see a gravel turnout where obviously other trucks have faced the same predicament, and I pull in there. Looking around, I decide the depth of the pullout, combined with the road, provides enough width for a U-turn. Because of the intermittent traffic, however, I probably couldn't complete the turn before a car came, and when I turned, I would block the entire road. Yet what else can I do? Still, I am afraid. A car speeding out of the night could easily smash into the trailer, possibly killing the driver. As I sit in my truck in the dark, worrying about what to do, I feel pressed hard against a wall with only one dangerous alternative, the U-turn.

I hate this. Why is this? Why wasn't the sign before the turn, warning me, instead of after? It's the nitwits sitting in offices making up rules they don't have to follow. They don't have to turn the truck around in the dark. As I apprehensively wrestle with this dilemma, traffic continues past, a car every minute or so. After a few minutes, a pickup stops beside my truck, and I think, *Now what?* The driver's side door opens, and the driver lifts out and up, turning over his truck's cab to face me. Shutting off the engine, I peer at this shadowy figure, an indiscernible face in the dark, and wonder what he wants.

"You don't have to turn here," I hear him say.

"Uh, what?" I ask, disbelievingly.

"You don't have to turn here. Go about two miles and just before the underpass, turn left. That will take you back to the main road."

I don't readily respond. *Is this a trick?* I cannot see the ghostly figure's face as I warily ask, "Is it okay for trucks to go that way?"

"Yes, it is."

"How will I know that I have the right road?"

"It's the only left turn between here and the bridge."

Wow! I can barely believe this and reply, "Thanks so much for stopping."

"That's okay," he says as he slips back into his pickup. He drives off into the dark, his taillights rapidly fading out of sight.

After he is gone, I start the truck and pull out of the gravel onto the blacktop. As I do, twin beams of light from an approaching car grow brighter, until those lights and mine, cross, mix, and separate as each of us speeds away from the other into the night.

Doing U-turns in a truck is extremely dangerous because the side of a truck broadside across a road is like a blank space that drivers often don't see. I know this and was scared as hell to do this turn, but what choice did I have? Fortunately for me, another angel came along.

BECAUSE I'M BLACK

At the Chicago Marshall Field's warehouse, the guard tells me to take the trailer to the lot across the street. As I enter the lot, I see a guard shack with a man inside who appears occupied with some task. To keep from blocking the entrance, I pull in a ways and stop. Getting out, I start to walk toward the guard shack to ask the guard where he wants the trailer dropped when another driver stops me.

"Did you have any trouble finding this place?" he asks.

"For sure, it is a bit tricky."

"Yeah, well, I got lost, and it was hell. I didn't think I would ever find it. Luckily though, I didn't meet any low underpasses."

"You were lucky, because they are all over the city."

As we talk, I am eager to check in but don't want to be rude. Meanwhile, the guard approaches us from the guard shack. My acquaintance, on seeing him, steps away to a truck parked nearby. When I turn to the guard, he addresses me.

"You thought he was in charge, didn't you?"

"What?" I say surprised, not sure of his meaning.

"You thought he was in charge, because he's white."

"Uh, no, we were just talking."

"You didn't think I was in charge, because I'm black."

"No, he just stopped me, and we were talking. I figured you were the guard, because you were in the guard shack."

"Yeah, but you went right to him."

"No, I didn't. I was on my way to the guard shack when he stopped me. I didn't want to be rude, so I talked to him for a moment."

"Yeah, sure," he replies, obviously not believing me.

Not wanting to continue this senseless argument, I said, "The guard across the street sent me over here to drop this trailer. Where would you like me to put it?"

"Over there," he says, motioning with his arm to an empty slot.

"Okay, thanks," I tell him, though he has already turned and walks away.

Yes, there's still prejudice, but this man has a huge chip on his shoulder that's crippling him.

SOMETHING ODD APPEARS

As I drive south on I-85 in Virginia through thick woods, the cloudy evening sky drops a light rain, a steady patter the wipers easily sweep away. As I scan ahead, something odd appears, something like fog but disturbing in its obvious denseness. Before I can decide what I see or what I should do, we collide: my truck and a wall of wind-driven rain. It floods the windshield, blinding me at sixty-five miles an hour. With an adrenaline rush, I brake hard, unsure if the road ahead is straight or curved, not knowing if I'm following the road or heading toward a precipice to fly into thin air and drop away to the bottom of a canyon.

The truck slows in a space of time that seems forever, until finally I manage to stop. The flooding continues five seconds, ten seconds, building my fear that a car bearing down on me will smash into my truck. Finally, the water parts, and I see a blurry path ahead of me. Starting out, I shift up, slowly dragging the heavy, loaded trailer to twenty-five, thirty-five, forty-five miles an hour as the fury around me subsides, and I again drive through a light steady patter.

WELL, THAT DRIVER IS PROBABLY...

My cell phone rings, and I recognize the number of another truck driver who regularly calls. We like talking back and forth, because it helps break up the long hours of driving. Reaching for the hands-free headset and positioning it on my head, I push the talk button on the phone just after the third ring, a habit of mine.

"Hello," I answer.

"Hi, what are you doing?"

"I'm stopped. I think there is an accident up ahead," I say.

"Where are you?"

"In Tennessee on I-40 east of Memphis. Where are you?"

"Florida. Uh-oh, there's a scale, and I have to go in. Gotta go."

"Okay."

My friend worked for my company but now drives a large Ford pickup pulling a flatbed trailer, hauling construction equipment. I wonder why the scale pulled him in. Well, he will probably call back and tell me.

I sit about thirty minutes before the traffic begins moving, cars and trucks backed up as far as I can see, both in front of and behind me. As the line steadily creeps along, the phone rings.

"How come they pulled you in?" I ask my friend, not bothering to say hello.

"Oh, I was driving along and swerved, you know, as we do sometimes. Only this time a state trooper, fast approaching from behind, spotted me. He called the scale and told them to pull me in, because he thought I was falling asleep."

"Well, were you?"

"No."

"So what happened?"

"They told me I had to drink a cup of coffee and, when I left there, stop at the first available motel."

"Did you?"

"I drank the coffee."

"I don't drink coffee. If I did that, I would be buzzing. Hey, I'm approaching the accident." As I talk, I roll slowly but steadily along. "I can't see much yet, but it's under an overpass. There is a tractor trailer, no, two tractor trailers. Damn! You should see this. Both trucks are sitting in the right lane under the overpass. The front truck's trailer broke in the middle, and the trailer's sagging in a V, almost touching the ground, so the rear of the trailer sticks up higher than normal. Wow! You will not believe where the end of that trailer rests. Probably both trucks ran sixty-five miles an hour with the second truck close behind. When the first truck stopped hard, who knows for what reason, possibly because the trailer spine snapped, the driver following had maybe two seconds before he drove under the trailer. The trailer sheared the cab above the engine, ramming through to the bunk."

My friend doesn't respond for a moment but then says, "Well, that driver is probably dead."

AND YOU

You like that little car, don't you. It zips. I can see that. You fly around, because, after all, your busy life demands a headlong rush to everywhere, and you cannot arrive there fast enough. Therefore, you zip by in your little car. You zip, and you watch, though not so much the other traffic. They are just indifferent obstacles to go around. No, you watch for your turn. It's somewhere along this four-lane, divided highway bordered on the right by a shopping center curb lined with parked cars and no shoulder. "Now where is that driveway? If only these damn trucks were not always in the way."

So you pass and pull in front of me and see your turn. Hitting your brakes, you nearly stop in front of an eighty-thousand-pound truck traveling fifty-five miles an hour—a vehicle that needs the length of a football field to stop. You hesitate and look for a way around another car that wants to exit, never considering what you just did: you gave up your life, and I cannot stop in time to save you.

In those fleeting seconds—all the time there ever is when life teeters on the edge—I look for a way out. Blocked by the curb and parked cars on the right and you in front, I instantly scan the left lane, surprisingly open. It's a lucky chance. In a blur I slip left, barely missing the rear of your car. You turn, zipping into the parking lot, zipping in without even knowing what you did, zipping in without the slightest awareness you came "that close" to dying. I promise you this: if there had been a car in the left lane, I would have hit you. I would not involve someone else in your accident. Yet, "hit" is a misnomer, for my truck would climb over your car, crushing it and you.

It's a fact that it takes a truck a longer distance to stop than a car. As I mentioned in the story, at fifty-five miles an hour a semi needs the length of a football field to stop. So if you stop in front of a truck going fifty-five, and less than a football field's length is between you, guess what is likely to happen if the truck is unable to change lanes?

THE DIFFERENCE BETWEEN RIGHT AND WRONG

At 2:00 a.m. in Birmingham, Alabama, I exit I-20, turn west onto US Highway 78, and drive one-half mile to the Pilot Truck Stop. There, even with sparse traffic, the light at the entrance stays red as though it will never change. As I sit in the dark waiting, I wonder if I'm watching a broken signal. Finally, the light does change. I turn into the truck stop and pull up to a fuel pump on the nearly deserted fuel island.

Climbing out, I insert my fuel card into the card reader and enter the required information. As my two ninety-gallon fuel tanks simultaneously fill from separate pumps on each side of the truck, I wash the windshield, side windows, and my seven mirrors. Completing fueling, I go inside for the fuel ticket. When I do, I notice the doughnut case, which tempts me to buy two doughnuts: a cake one with chocolate frosting, and a glazed, raspberry-filled one.

With my doughnuts, I return to my truck and do the necessary paperwork before exiting the truck stop and turning west on Highway 78. As I leave town, I relax and think now I will have a doughnut. In the dark I cannot see them and just take one from the sack, which sits on the floor beside my seat. I left the top of the sack open so I could easily reach down and pick up a doughnut. I don't know which doughnut I have and it doesn't matter. With expectation, I bite into it. Immediately I know something is wrong. Clicking on the reading light over the door, I see the problem. I eat the doughnut upside down with the frosting on the bottom instead of the top where it belongs. That this should matter surprises me. Yet I have to admit I always eat doughnuts right side up. Smiling at myself, I turn the doughnut over and eat it right side up. After all, I know the difference between right and wrong.

DO YOU KNOW WHAT I WOULD REALLY LIKE TO HAVE?

At 1:00 a.m., I am at the Little America Inn and Truck Stop at Flagstaff, Arizona. It is five days until Christmas. Pushing open the door to the convenience store, I enter at the diesel fuel desk and head to the snack section near the rear of the store. First, though, I pass through four or five aisles of gifts, various interesting items, which attract my attention, and I begin browsing. There are fancy note cards and envelopes in ornate boxes, luxuriously soft leather jackets, crystal figurines and hearts, bone-handled knives with bronze trim, carved pottery vases and bowls, fancy watches, natural-bristle back-scrubbing brushes, prickly pear cactus candy, wild huckleberry Gummy Bears, cranberry-and-lemon-rind exfoliating body polish, and on and on.

I wander the isles, pausing many times to inspect some new discovery. Reaching the magazine rack, I stop to check out the latest celebrity gossip. As I scan the headlines, a man stops with his back to me in the next aisle. He catches my eye—his straggly gray-streaked hair, his sheepskin jacket—and I study him for a moment before returning to reading. Then, before I realize he is there, he stands beside me, surprising me.

"Do you know what I would really like to have?" he says. He's standing confidently close to me as though we are old friends temporarily separated in the store by different interests.

"What would you really like to have?" I respond, curious to what he would choose out of the myriad choices. He returns to where I first saw him, and I follow. With his back to me, he reaches for something and turns to me holding a three-pack of Gillette "Good News" single-use razor blades. I am so surprised, I laugh.

Without a word, he puts the razors back and walks away. Before he does, I see a sad, vacant face, and through my mind flash images of failed marriages and failed jobs. I sense he is lost, to the point where he approaches a stranger at one o'clock in the morning to ask, "Do you know what I would really like to have?"

I KNOW WHERE YOUR WHEEL IS

When I stop at Primm, Nevada, on a Friday evening for a casino buffet, the sun hangs low in the sky. Later, stars shine in the first hour of the night as I leave Primm, headed east toward Las Vegas. Moderately heavy traffic surrounds me, weekenders out of the Los Angeles basin who hurry to the glitz and gambling. Suddenly a black mound two to three feet high appears close in front of the truck, and before I can react, I hit it.

Startled, I steady the truck, steer onto the shoulder, and stop, unsure what happened. Shutting off the engine, I climb out to investigate and smell the strong odor of diesel fuel. Taking a flashlight from the driver's door pocket, I bend down to look under the truck. There I discover a car tire mounted on a rim, jammed against the driver's side fuel tank. Fuel pours from the damaged tank in a steady stream onto the ground, and I don't see any way to stop it. The tank holds ninety gallons of diesel fuel, and spills are serious business.

Returning to my cab, I send a Qualcomm message reporting the accident and seeking help. Again getting out, I take my safety triangles from the side box and set them up behind the truck. That's when I notice a car towing a van stopped on the shoulder several hundred feet behind me and two men standing by the driver's side front wheel. Curious, I walk back, wondering if the wheel under my truck belongs to them. When I reach the van, I notice the missing tire and wheel on the front driver's side of the van. In addition, I see that when the wheel came off, it damaged the hub.

"Hi, I know where your wheel is," I say, addressing the two men. "It's jammed under my truck against a fuel tank, and diesel fuel is spilling onto the ground." The two Hispanic men look at me rather perplexed, and I am not sure they understood what I said.

Finally, one of them responds, "You have our wheel?"

"Yes, I hit it, and it's under my truck."

"We cannot put it back on," he says, looking at the hub.

"No, I don't think you can," I agree.

He speaks in Spanish to his friend, and they begin unhooking the van from the car and pay no more attention to me. Taking my notepad from my pocket, I write down the make of the car and the license number. As I walk back to my truck, they pass me in their car, and I watch their taillights disappear in the dark. Thirty minutes elapse since I sent the Qualcomm message, and now a patrol car with two officers pulls up behind my truck, their car's red lights flashing a warning into the night. Leaving his car, one officer approaches me, standing behind my truck.

"What's the problem, driver?" he asks me. I describe what happened, and he says, "You will have to move your truck farther off the road."

I correctly parked on the asphalt shoulder, not overlapping the white line, although I'm edging it. However, cars and trucks not moving left pass dangerously close. Because of the narrow shoulder, though, to move the truck over would put the passenger-side tires onto the sloping gravel bank. This would tilt the heavy load stacked high in the trailer, possibly causing the truck to roll over and down the bank. Still, something else concerns me, and I respond to the officer. "You want me to start up my truck with diesel fuel soaking the ground underneath and move farther onto the shoulder? No way," I say firmly. "That truck stays right there."

Only later do I consider that moving the truck would have extended the fuel spill to a larger area. The officer does not persist, and soon a fire truck with four fire fighters arrives, and I repeat my story. The fire fighters check out the leaking tank, yet none of them tries to stop the leak. Instead they just mill around, for, after all, this is not a fire. Soon an insurance specialist arrives, and I again tell my story as he completes his report. Then a hazmat specialist arrives in cheery spirits, because his company will clean up the spill; it's an expensive undertaking, for they have to remove and treat many yards of soil. Meanwhile another patrol car arrives. After him comes a mechanic from a truck stop near Las Vegas. We now have enough for a party. With all the flashing lights, passersby slow down and gawk.

The first officer needs to complete his paperwork, so I climb into the backseat of the patrol car, behind the two officers. The officer asks me an occasional question as he fills in his form. He also talks to the other officer. They exchange stories of hunting trips, women, and who did what to whom. I tell him I wrote down the license number of the car pulling the van, but he doesn't pay attention. Eventually he completes his report. Exasperated by now, I ask him, "Don't you want the license number of the car pulling the van?"

"Do you have it?" he asks.

"Yes, I do," I say and give it to him. He excuses me, and I get out of the patrol car. Now that the bureaucratic parade has completed their paperwork, they all leave, having done nothing. The officers who first arrived found the name and address in Las Vegas of the man who owns the car pulling the van, and they go to find him. With just the mechanic and me left, he checks out the leak and finds the tank nearly empty.

"We will probably have to take your truck to the shop to fix it," he says.

"What about the leaking fuel?" I ask.

"Well, it's not too bad, and you have enough fuel in the other tank to make it to the truck stop."

I think, *I know there is enough fuel in the second tank to reach the truck stop. But what about the fuel under my truck when I start up the truck, and what about this hazmat fuel spill regimen I endured these past few hours? How can I drive to the truck stop spilling fuel along the highway?* I don't say any of this, because I am tired of the whole rigmarole. Instead, I obediently follow the mechanic down the interstate to the truck stop, all the while leaking diesel fuel along the highway.

A MOMENT OF PEACE

Having parked at the Franklin, Kentucky, Flying J, I decide to buy something to eat from the convenience store. On approaching the back of the building from the parking lot, I notice a disheveled man with a small pack standing in an alcove. He looks at me as I pass by. When I return, on the way back to my truck, he is still there. This time he speaks to me.

"Would you be going to Louisville?" he asks me in a quiet, nervous way, his shoulders slumped. "I am sick, and I need to go home."

I stop to answer, lying, "No, I'm not." I'm not supposed to pick up hitchhikers. When I start to step away, he behaves desperately and hurries to ask me, "Could you spare some money so I can eat? I need to take my medicine," he says, taking a pill bottle from his coat pocket and showing it to me in the palm of his hand. "I have to take them with food." I look closely at him, and he looks sick.

Without hesitation, I take out my wallet and give him five dollars. Later I wish I'd given him more. Still, why would I give him money anyway? Because I know life can be hard. Even though he could well be conning me, I do not want to judge him. I can spare the money so when asked, I give it. In the past, I couldn't. A friend of mine won't give money but instead buys panhandlers food, because he doesn't want them to buy alcohol or cigarettes.

When I look at this trampled man with his pill bottle, I think, *This poor soul scrapes along the bottom of nowhere.* Shouldn't he be able to choose whether he has a sandwich, a cigarette, or a beer? Is there nothing left to him? Am I not giving him the money to help him? Does it matter what he does with it? Not to me. Besides, five dollars won't keep him from starvation, while a cigarette or a beer may give him a moment of peace.

SHE DOESN'T DO IT ON PURPOSE, JUST OUT OF IGNORANCE

At the first exit on I-25 in Cheyenne, Wyoming, I loop over the interstate to reach the flying J Truck Stop. Once across the bridge, I meet construction, a jungle of equipment, orange cones, and torn-up asphalt. A young woman with an orange vest stands in the road directing traffic to the right around the corner. She intends for me to follow the cars in front of me. They easily round the corner, yet I must swing wide to clear the curb. However, she stands in the path I need to follow, forcing me to cut the corner short. I don't want to do this, yet she refuses to budge, even though I come as close to her as I safely can. It isn't enough. The trailer rides up and over the curb, and the two outside trailer tires rub against a slightly protruding metal utility box buried in the ground. As the tires drag against the box, *pop, pop,* both tires blow out.

A HARD TIME

As I approach Tulsa, Oklahoma, at three o'clock in the afternoon, several thin trails of black smoke rise into the sky. A few miles farther, I encounter a grass fire alongside the road, the orange flames steadily moving forward, consuming the dry, weathered blades as the blackened area behind the flames steadily grows. *Hmm, how did that start?* I wonder. Maybe a motorist tossed out a lit cigarette butt that rolled on the blacktop and ended up on the edge of the shoulder where it ignited the dry grass.

Passing the fire, I dismiss it from my mind, but several hundred yards down the road, another fire licks at some brush, surprising me. Farther on, another fire climbs a bank toward some sheds, where a man sprays water from a hose. *What is going on here?* I don't know.

Two miles past the fires, I approach exit fourteen where the three o'clock start of rush hour traffic slows to near fifty-five miles an hour. Because of congestion at that exit, I move into the left lane. Now, ahead of me stretches open space, plenty of room to stop before reaching the next car. Beside me, six or seven cars occupy the right lane, including a Tulsa police cruiser without its lights on. It paces the traffic. Suddenly the officer cuts in front of me, turning on his lights and coming to a near stop. *Damn, what is he doing?*

I brake, knowing I cannot go right, and one glance left tells me the truck will roll in the median. Holding the wheel steady to avoid a jackknife, I hope I can stop in time. Yet the cruiser's lights only blink twice before I hit the heavy sedan with a hard *thump*, jerking it two or three times on its springs and shocks. As both our vehicles settle to a stop, a dark feeling overcomes me. *Oh no, damn, I'm in trouble. He cut me off. Yeah, right, but he's a cop, and I hit him.*

A moment later, the patrol car slowly turns back across the right lane, and I follow, the other traffic giving way, allowing us to pull up onto the end of exit fourteen's ramp. Once stopped, I wait as two officers exit the cruiser to stand behind their car examining the damage, which I am hard-pressed to see. It looks like there is a dent in the bumper and a slight crease on the trunk lid. The younger officer, whom I identify as the driver, leaves his partner and approaches my truck. As he does, I roll down the window.

"Let me have your driver's license," he directs me.

I hand him my license, and he takes it and walks away. Meanwhile two more patrol cars arrive, the officers exiting their respective vehicles and milling around, each inspecting the damaged car. Two of the officers cross the now-slowed westbound lanes, looking, I suppose, for skid marks. Probably there won't be any because of the tractor trailer's antilock brakes. I notice the third officer speaking with the cruiser's driver and his partner, and I assume he is the investigating officer. Shortly, he approaches me.

"I need your registration," he tells me. When I give it to him, he returns to his car. Soon he is back and commanding me, "Now, tell me what happened."

I tell him the cruiser changed lanes, cutting in front of me and stopping, not allowing enough room to avoid hitting him. Only later do I discover the police report states the cruiser was in front of me with its lights on, trying to cross the median, and I rear-ended it. There isn't any mention that the officer changed lanes, cutting me off without enough room to stop. Thus, the report implies I followed the cruiser too closely, and that's why I rear-ended it.

"Under the present conditions, you were driving too fast, or you would not have hit the patrol car," the investigating officer tells me.

"What conditions?" I ask.

"With fires and emergency vehicles in the area, you should have been driving more slowly," he responds.

"The nearest fire is two miles away, behind us, and any emergency vehicles are on the other side of the interstate, headed east to the fires," I answer him. Yet he doesn't listen. When he hands me the ticket, I see he wrote on it, "speed affecting conditions," and "failure to stop assured clear distance." As I study the ticket, he explains how to comply with it. As he does, I continue to study the ticket and notice something weird. He listed the two officers involved in the accident as witnesses. How can that be? How can they be witnesses? I thought witnesses were independent observers. How can a police officer be his own witness?

The next day when I tell the story to my friend, another driver, he responds, "The company will fire you. You can't pay the ticket; you need to get a lawyer."

"I didn't do anything wrong. If I hadn't remained calm, the accident might have been much worse. I did the only thing I could: stop as soon as possible. Can't I just go to court and tell the judge that?"

"No way, you don't know the law. You have to get a lawyer. Even then, you will probably lose."

In the next few days, my friend hammers at me, "You have to get a lawyer." So, using my laptop, which has a wireless connection, I find a Tulsa attorney willing to represent me. She will attend the first court appearance on my behalf and ask for a trial date. Meanwhile it has been ten days since the accident. I continue to run loads, though now dispatch assigns me a load picking up at the Springfield, Ohio, terminal. There, most likely, safety will pull me in as standard procedure to write up an accident report, even though I previously phoned one in. Sure enough, when I reach the terminal, the guard tells me to report to safety. Once inside I sign up and wait. Soon an affable-looking older man calls my name, and I follow him into his office.

"Hi, how are you?" he greets me pleasantly.

Well, at least he isn't a hard-faced asshole, though just the same, I know he has a job to do. Still I believe he will be nice about it, not judgmental and degrading.

"Hi, I'm okay, thanks," I respond.

In the next few minutes, which seem like forever, he intently studies the computer screen while working the keyboard, and I wonder what he could be typing.

After a while he pauses and, turning to me, says, "Is that for me?" He's referring to a sheet of paper I hold, on which I have written my version of the accident.

"Uh, yes, it is," I answer, handing it to him.

Briefly reading it, he again types into the computer. Then he activates the printer, which feeds out a copy, and he reads to me a condensed description of the accident. "Is that right?" he asks.

"Yeah, sure," I tell him.

Apparently satisfied, he says, "Please go out into the reception area and wait."

"Okay," I say.

A few minutes later, he calls me back. When I enter the room, another safety officer, a young man with spiked hair, awaits me. The older man introduces us and, though I miss his name, I cannot help noticing his edginess, his sharp awareness. Just the same, I remain calm as the three of us take our seats.

"I just spoke with the main office, and you are indefinitely suspended," the first officer tells me as the young man watches.

The words hit me with a punch, slamming me emotionally backward. I wasn't prepared for that. I am shocked, numbed, for "indefinitely suspended" is a hairbreadth short of fired.

"You cannot leave the terminal unless you have all the company's property removed from your truck, which includes the base plate." Then I couldn't legally drive the truck on the street. "I am sorry," he says, and I believe him. "I was just on the phone with the safety officer handling your case, and you can call and talk to him if you like. Do you want me to give you the number?"

"What's the point?" *Why would I want to bang my head against a brick wall?*

Still, he insists. "Here, let me write it on my card for you." Afterward, he hands me the card, which I put into my shirt pocket.

Back in my truck, I numbly lie on the bed, wondering what to do.

The company has stranded me nineteen hundred miles from home in Phoenix, Arizona, and I cannot legally drive my truck back to Phoenix. Even if I get a temporary permit, the fuel will cost $750 to drive that far.

Why have they done this? Certainly I hit the patrol car and am responsible for that; however, I didn't have a reasonable alternative. It just seems as though that's it. It doesn't matter how irresponsible the officer was. By his actions, he risked many lives. What's more, he couldn't cross the median there; it was impassable. Why didn't he just use the ramp? The whole affair doesn't make any sense. Although a rear-end collision is serious, this accident was not. I just didn't consider that the cruiser might pull in front of me and stop. I should have planned an escape route.

What am I going to do? No other company will hire me with a rear-end accident on my record. Easy now, take it easy, don't panic. Shit! Son of a bitch, I will be destitute! I cannot get some shit job paying minimum wage. I can't live on that. I can't pay my bills. I can't do this, and I cannot ask anyone for help. My friends and family have their own problems. This feels like the end of the line. Easy, man, easy, I tell myself. As I lie on the bed, I feel heavy, barely able to move, flattened. Then I remember the attorney. I had better call the attorney.

"I have been fired," I tell her, "or more correctly, indefinitely suspended. Yet it feels like I'm fired, and my truck is locked in the terminal."

"Oh no, I'm sorry," she sympathizes.

"Safety gave me the number of some guy in the main office and said I should call him, but I don't see the point, but hey, maybe you could call him?"

"Certainly, give me his number, and I will call you back after I talk to him."

"Okay," I agree.

Fifteen minutes later, she rings me back and says, "I just talked to him, and he is a bit of an ass. He said that no matter what, you are responsible, even though I pointed out to him that when someone cuts in front of you, it doesn't always work out that way. I told him I would be representing you to the court next Wednesday, and he said to keep him posted as to the outcome."

After we hang up, I feel half-frozen, not cold but immobile. I think, *Come on now, you can get through this. Fight, don't roll over and play dead. Wow, I feel so tired, and I could sure use a shower.* I wonder if I can still get a shower, now that I am persona non grata, but hey, I'm probably overreacting. I anticipate the receptionist possibly turning me away, but she doesn't. Once showered, I feel better.

As I exit the building, however, a snow flurry blows down from the sky, probably a last burst of winter before spring. This worries me because now I must run my truck to stay warm, and I fear I will run out of fuel, for idling burns a gallon per hour. They have fuel pumps at the terminal, but most likely the company cut off my fuel card. Therefore, I shut the engine off until the cold chills me and restart it until again warm, continuing the cycle repeatedly. I don't know what I will do when I run out of fuel. While considering this, my phone rings; it is my driver friend.

"Hello," I offer.

"How're you doing?"

"Not so good," I tell him and relate the events concerning my suspension. "It feels like I have been fired. I don't know what I am going to do. I can't drive back to Phoenix. It's too expensive, and I am afraid to leave my truck here. They might tow it. I have heard of drivers leaving their trucks at our terminals, say, after an accident, and when they returned, all of their personal belongings were stolen. Who knows by whom, maybe even by other drivers? I think the best thing I can do is to just stay here and wait until the ticket is resolved. Yet that could take weeks, maybe even months."

"No, you can't leave your truck," my friend agrees. "That's a bad idea, and what about your car?" He means my 1999 Corvette parked at the Phoenix, Arizona, terminal in its driver's parking lot. "They might have that towed, too."

"Yeah, I know. But what should I do?"

"Call the terminal manager and ask him if he thinks it will be towed."

"I guess I could. That's a good idea."

"Call me back."

"Okay."

The terminal manager tells me, "Don't worry about it. No one is going to tow it."

Hearing that is a big relief. I call my driver friend and tell him. Afterward, I check my e-mail and find the following message from my attorney:

Vernon,
I just wanted to let you know I will be going to court on Wednesday morning, and I will talk to the prosecutor regarding what we can do. It is possible he will dismiss the case (somewhat unlikely). If not, we will need to get a trial date. If that happens, I will get a copy of the tape from the police car (each car has a camera installed in it). In addition, I will try to get a copy of any driving incidents contained within the officer's personnel record. I am sorry you have to deal with all of this, especially with your employer being so unsupportive.
Best regards,
P

By Wednesday, the temperature warms up considerably. This relieves me, because now I only need to run the engine to charge the battery. While I wait for the much-anticipated call from the attorney, I fuss around on the computer until I receive her call at 10:30 a.m.

"I have good news," she says excitedly. "If you do twelve hours of community service, the court will dismiss the ticket."

"That's great!" I say.

"I got the earliest court date I could, April 12. Do you think you can complete the work by then?"

"I suppose so. I'll figure something out," I tell her. I hang up and think, *I will need a car.*

Another driver informs me our company has a special arrangement with Avis and that the courtesy van will take me to the Avis rental office. I do that and drive a Dodge Stratus back to the terminal. Once there, I consult the yellow pages to find the Volunteer Service Bureau of Clark County. A young woman answers, and I say, "Hi, this is Vernon Sheperd. I had a minor accident with a police officer, and the court will forgive the ticket if I do twelve hours of community service."

"Not all our organizations will accept court-ordered community-service volunteers," she tells me.

Yeah, people forced to do community service probably lack enthusiasm or, worse, need babysitting. After a few of those, the organizations become reluctant to take court-ordered volunteers. Just the same, she comes up with American Cancer Society, Red Cross, Humane Society, Waste Management, and the Family Service Center. Calling several of them, I run into resistance: So-and-so will call you, or he is busy or away from his desk or whatever. "So-and-so" never calls. After a couple days of this, I get through to Kris at the Humane Society, and she says, "Yes, we can always use help, especially of the male persuasion. Some of the women are just, 'Oh, that's so stinky.' Can you work tomorrow and Saturday and be here at eight o'clock? I have two people out sick."

"Yeah, sure, I'll be there," I promise her.

Over the next couple of days, I clean dog pens, wash walls and woodwork, and weed flowerbeds. At the end of it, Kris writes on my paperwork, "Vernon did a great job for us." I mail the completed forms to the attorney and, over the next days before the April 12 court date, I look for ways to pass the time.

Now that I have the rental car, I decide to get out and do something to keep from going nuts, to distract my mind. Checking the Ohio map, I locate Brown Reservoir on the outskirts of Springfield, probably less than ten miles from the terminal, an easy trip. I spend a day there, walking, sitting, just relaxing in the summer sun. A couple of days later, I visit the Cedar Bog Nature Preserve north of Springfield, best described as a swamp. Following a wooden pathway built by volunteers, I discover spring wildflowers beginning to bloom. The next day

I go to an antique mall a mile from the terminal, as I like to explore such places.

One day I decide to contact other trucking companies, inquiring about a driving job. Yet all the companies I call dismiss me. "We cannot hire you if your company reports your accident as chargeable. You have to clear that up before we will consider your application." I anticipated this, but still it hammers me.

Finally, it is April 12 and the second court date, and I nervously await the attorney's call. She still has not called by 4:00 p.m. so I call her office. The receptionist tells me, "She is out and not expected back today." Damn! Why didn't she call? Well, I am not her only client. Yeah, that's probably it; she's just busy.

The following morning she does call. "I am sorry I didn't get back to you yesterday; my workload buried me. The court dismissed the ticket, and I called the safety officer at your company and told him, asking if they would reinstate you. He said no, but he might let you come to the main terminal for a skills evaluation and, depending on the outcome, they might reinstate you. I am sorry. I will send him a letter stating the court's decision and encouraging him to reinstate you, though I doubt it will do any good."

"Thanks. At least the court dismissed the ticket; that's something. Thank you for your help."

"You're welcome. I'm sorry I couldn't do more. The next time you're in Tulsa, call me, and I will buy you lunch."

"That would be great, thanks. Good-bye."

"Good-bye."

I sit in my truck depressed and wonder why I bothered. I could have just paid the ticket and saved all of this time and money. Still, it seems as though the canceled ticket remains a fragile thread keeping me from falling into an abyss, for the company has not officially fired me. Maybe I still have a chance. I had better go into the office tomorrow and talk to Safety.

The following morning, the receptionist checks my file in the computer and tells me I need to see Safety. Clearly some decision has been made. When the receptionist finally calls me, and I go to the indicated office, I find the spike-haired safety officer.

"You need to talk to the main office," he tells me, reaching for the phone and dialing.

I don't want to talk to them, no way, but it looks like I don't have a choice.

"I have Vernon Sheperd here in the office with me," the safety officer tells the officer at the main office.

"Yes, of course," I hear him reply, for the speakerphone is turned on.

"Well, Mr. Sheperd, why did you come back?"

"Uh, I am not sure what you mean. I never left."

"He has been here since March 24 (three weeks)," the Springfield safety officer interjects, and for a moment, the room is silent.

What is going on here? I think.

Finally I hear, "We will allow you to come to the main terminal for a skills evaluation, and, depending on the outcome, you may be reinstated. However, you must bobtail here at your own expense. You cannot pull a load, but we will arrange for a temporary transit permit. What would you like to do?"

I wonder, *Why do I need a transit permit. My truck still has all its permits*, but I answer, "Okay, I will do that."

"Then you will need to call the owner-operator manager."

"Okay."

I don't understand why I need to call him, but okay, I will. Later that afternoon I reach Jeff, the owner-operator manager, after several calls to a busy line or a "he is away from his desk" response. Identifying myself, I inform him, "I was told to call you, that I would need a temporary transit permit. Why? I still have all my permits."

Surprising me, he answers, "You called me. You told me you quit."

I'm surprised and shocked and think, *What the hell?* "I never called you. I never told you I quit. Someone might have called you, but it wasn't me."

"You told me you quit. I canceled all of your permits. Why were you told to call me?"

"I am to go to the main terminal for a skills evaluation. Apparently, I need a transit permit to do that."

"I will have to check on this. Call back later."

"Okay."

I'll be damned! They had me out the door, and I didn't even know it. Obviously, they didn't need to fire me. They just conveniently had me quit, shuffled me off. But I didn't go away. If I had, that might have been the end of it, for once the door closes, how do you open it again? Well, what the hell, I need to go to the main terminal. That is the only possible way out of this mess.

When I tell my driver friend what transpired, he replies, "They don't want to pay unemployment, and if you quit, they don't have to. They have their records, and the owner-operator manager will swear you told him you quit."

"I can't believe that. It's just too underhanded. Besides, I thought the state pays unemployment. It's probably just a misunderstanding. Yet it doesn't make any sense. Why reevaluate me? I will still go to the main terminal, though I don't know exactly what I will have to do, and it worries me, but what choice do I have? At least I have a chance to get my job back."

Later I again get through to Jeff after several calls, and arrangements are made for a temporary transit permit.

Several days later, I arrive at the main terminal, having taken my time, driving cautiously and not pushing myself, because I don't have insurance, because that was also canceled. Reporting to Safety, I find myself thrust into the constant crush of the company's hiring of new drivers needed to stopgap the bleed, the 80 percent (or so I have been told) turnover of new drivers the first year. As a result, I wait a long time, taking my turn with several dozen others. Eventually, my turn comes.

A Safety Officer tells me, "You will have to complete 'e-training' (computer classes), a simulator course, and take a road test. On completing them, a decision will be made as to whether you will be reinstated."

The e-training is a snap. I receive 90 to 100 percent on all the dozen or so classes assigned me. After all, I have driven for over ten years. The road test is a bit hairy, because my truck has a super-ten transmission, and the test truck is a standard ten-speed. So I grind a few gears, though, in the end, I pass.

The simulator requires more explanation. The company converted a Freightliner Century into a simulator, much like that used to train pilots, except, of course, those are planes instead of trucks. The principle is the same. The truck, placed in a building, is attached to computers that project a scene onto the truck's windshield, depending on whatever scenario is programmed. It looks just like a real truck. It is a real truck. You start it up and shift it, driving down the road, encountering obstacles such as sharp turns, railroad tracks, accidents, low underpasses, snowstorms, etc., any conditions a driver might experience on the road. Yet, of course, the truck never leaves the building.

Two drivers are tested alternately with each session only lasting a few minutes, because the computer can hammer a driver with many hazards and problems, causing a high level of stress. The testing officer decides on the level of difficulty for each driver. The driver testing with me joined the company three months ago and rolled his truck in a snowstorm in Wyoming. The control station, where the testing officer sits, contains a screen showing what the tested driver experiences and his reactions. The other driver does not have my level of skill, so his tests are less difficult than mine. We each have three sessions, and I finish with a slam-banger.

The scene begins at night in a snowstorm on an entrance ramp. I ease the truck into gear, starting up the ramp, and the blacktop appears shiny, possibly with black ice. I cannot feel the road, because the truck is not actually on blacktop.

As I cautiously pick up speed on the ramp, all the while watching for other vehicles, the snowstorm turns into a near whiteout. Merging onto the interstate, the truck begins jackknifing, and I counter, turning the steering wheel to compensate. However, I overcorrect, and the trailer swings the other way. I correct again, struggling to control the truck and avoid a jackknife. Yet, a gust of wind slams the trailer, forcing the truck right and into a snow-covered field. As I frantically steer back toward the interstate, the truck slips and slides, this way and that until, finally, I guide the truck onto the highway. Again, gusts of wind hammer the truck, and again I fight to keep from jackknifing or rolling. With quick corrections, I counter, keeping the truck upright; however, I plunge into the median. Plowing through piles of drifted snow, I reach the other side of the highway where, rolling to a stop, I block both lanes.

Whoa! I have to get out of here before someone slams into me. Engaging the clutch, I try to move. Still another gust hits the truck, forcing it into a jackknife. The wind slowly pushes the cab back into a tight V as I desperately attempt to correct with the steering to no avail. The nose nearly touches the trailer before stopping. Damn, I'm stuck! There is no way to pull out of this; that's it. The windshield goes blank, and the session is over. Afterward, the testing officer tells me, "I hit you with a seventy-mile-an-hour wind. There wasn't anything you could do about that."

Much later, after again waiting my turn, I face the safety officer.

"You successfully completed the skills evaluation and are reinstated. However, you are on six months' probation, and if you experience any problems during that time, you will most likely be terminated."

All right, I have my job back! Yes! I can do this!

THE JOURNEY HOME

Navajo country in northern Arizona—a rugged, eye-striking landscape of plateaus and jutting cliffs in various shades of rust red—passes by outside my truck windows. With the daylight nearly gone, a light, gusting wind picks up sand and dust, the possible beginnings of a sandstorm. Arriving at US Highway 160, a junction in the high desert with no facilities, I see a young man thumbing a ride headed my way. As I turn onto highway 160 and pass him, I look back in my mirror. I see him make a desperate, praying motion with his hands. I think he is saying, "Please stop." I hitchhiked before and imagine myself stranded there, where he will probably spend the night. Does he have a sleeping bag? I don't know.

I brake, and when I finally stop, he has a ways to walk. That's okay. He won't mind. I reach over the seat, open the door, and wait until he peers up at me from the shoulder of the road.

"Thanks for stopping. I'm going to Farmington."

"Farmington, where is that?"

"In New Mexico," he says.

"I turn north at Kayenta, about a hundred or so miles from here, but I can take you that far."

"Okay," he responds.

"Hand me your pack." He hands his pack up to me with a slightly curved board attached to it and, yes, he does have a sleeping bag. Once he is seated, I show him how he can adjust his seat to make the ride more comfortable. He doesn't offer his name, and I don't ask. Instead, as I shift into gear and start moving off, I say, "What's in Farmington?"

"My grandparents live there and my uncle."

"Oh, so you are going for a visit?"

"No, I live with my grandparents. My mom ran away when I was really small, and my grandparents raised me."

"Do you have brothers or sisters?" I ask.

"No, there is no one else, just my grandparents, my uncle, and me," he replies.

When he says that, a scene flashes in my mind of a nephew's recent high school graduation, where perhaps fifty relatives and friends gushed with admiration and support for that young man.

"And your dad, what about him?" I ask.

"Don't know. My grandparents were like my mom and dad, so I never really missed anything."

Never missed anything? Yes, you did. You missed having both parents and grandparents.

"Are you a Christian?"

"Yes, I am," he responds with surprise. "Why do you ask?"

"Because I saw you making that praying motion with your hands."

"Yes, I am a Christian. My grandfather is a minister."

His grandfather is a minister, I think disbelievingly. Now can you picture what a minister's son might look like? I can, square as a waffle and wimpy as a noodle. Having said that I can hear all the ministers' sons of the world calling for my head. Yet, he isn't. He's in his twenties, weight about 150 pounds, five foot ten inches tall, with dark hair and a dark complexion. He's confident but not overbearing, just secure in himself. He's also polite, pleasant, modest, and not contentious, unlike many young men his age. I bet women consider him attractive.

I change the subject and ask, "What is that board you are carrying?"

"It's a snowboard. I was snowboarding up in Oregon."

Suddenly a gust of wind slams the truck, grabbing my attention, and we ride in silence for a while. The wind buffets the truck, and swirling masses of dust and sand obscure the road as dark overtakes us. I slow down and, after a while, pick up the conversation, wondering aloud, "Do you often hitchhike?"

"No, this is my first time, and everyone has been really nice. I had a ride with another trucker to where you picked me up. I have been thinking about going to truck-driving school," he said.

"How old are you?" I ask.

"I'm twenty-four."

"How is your driving record? Any tickets or accidents?"

"No, no accidents or tickets or anything."

"Do you have a police record, especially any felonies?" I say.

"No, nothing like that," he says.

"How about your work record? What work have you done since high school?"

"I was in the Job Corps, and for the last four years, I worked for my uncle in construction."

"Well, you sound like a good candidate to me," I say. As we push on through the sandstorm, the conversation again stalls. He sits quietly, staring out into the night as jolting gusts of dust and sand rock the truck, hampering my ability to see and keeping my attention focused on the road. After an hour and a half, I know the turnoff has to be near. Peering intently through the dark, I apprehensively strain to see, because I dread turning around if I miss it.

"We should be getting close to where I have to let you off," I offer. He glances at me but does not respond. Ahead I spot a red light and, as I approach, I recognize a highway marker. Stopping at the light, I say to him, "Let me turn first, and I will drop you on the other side."

I do not want to put him out in this nasty sandstorm. Fortunately there are a couple of fast-food restaurants at this junction, and they are still open. At least he will have temporary shelter. Maneuvering around the corner, I look for a place to pull off. There isn't much room, but there isn't much traffic either. I pull off as far as I can, though I overlap into the street. I stop, turn off the truck, and turn on my four-ways. With the cab now quiet, he asks me a question.

"Could you spare a dollar? I lost my water bottle and need to buy another one."

"Uh, just a minute," I respond. *If he doesn't have money for a bottle of water, he doesn't have money for food either, and he won't arrive home until late tomorrow*, I think. As he opens the door to climb out, I caution him, "Be sure to use all the handholds," for you can easily fall getting out of a tractor trailer. He does and, when he is securely on the ground, I hand him his pack and say, "Hold on a second." Folding a five-dollar bill, I hand it down to him. He takes the bill and unfolds it.

"No way," he snaps at me.

"Yes, way," I shoot back.

He hesitates before replying, "Thanks and bless you." All the while, the nasty dirt and dust swirl around and over him, the truck offering little protection. He closes the door and hurries away, disappearing into the murky dark as I watch and think *He will be home tomorrow.*

Putting the truck in gear, I cautiously edge onto the road as an impatient driver wheels around me, and a heavy swirl of dust temporarily blocks my vision. *What the hell, how can he see when I can't?* I should stop, but there isn't anywhere to park. I slowly drive on until, after a few minutes, the visibility improves, and I increase my speed. Eventually the night is still, and I push on through the dark. When I reach I-40, I am out of hours and must park. The gravel shoulder is wide enough, so I park there. Putting up the black privacy curtain, I sit in the driver's seat to complete my logbook, finishing my workday. Now I get to go home, just like everyone else. Well, not quite like everyone else. I rise out of the seat, step back into the sleeper, undress, set the timer for eight hours, and climb into my bunk. In a few minutes, I fall asleep.

GLOSSARY OR THINGS YOU SHOULD KNOW TO BETTER UNDERSTAND THE STORIES

Bobtail or BT: A tractor without a trailer. This also means to drive from one location to another without a trailer.

Bridge law: Complicated, confusing laws few people understand that regulate the allowable distance between the fifth-wheel pin and the rear axles, which is different for each state.

Bull hauler: A driver of a tractor trailer combination with a metal, cage-like trailer used to haul farm animals such as cattle, pigs, and chickens.

Cab-over: A flat-fronted tractor with the engine under the cab.

CB: Citizens-band radio, how truck drivers communicate with one another other than cell phone.

Condo: A high-rise, double-bunk tractor.

Cracker: A four-wheel driver who cuts through the crack created when one vehicle passes another.

Deadhead or DH: To travel with an empty trailer. Also, the distance traveled while empty.

Dock and/or dock door: A door opening on a warehouse that facilitates the transfer of goods from the trailer into the warehouse. Usually there is a rubber pad on each side of the dock opening, which cushions the impact of the trailer against the warehouse.

DOT: An acronym for the Department of Transportation, which regulates commercial vehicles.

Drive tires: The two axles and eight tires on the rear of a tractor.

Dry van: An enclosed trailer that hauls dry goods as opposed to refrigerated goods.

Empty or MT: An empty trailer.

Fifth wheel: The black, wheel-like unit containing a locking device, which attaches to and secures the pin on the trailer. The greased fifth wheel allows the trailer to pivot smoothly on the pin as the tractor turns right or left.

Four-wheeler: Any four-wheel vehicle, including cars and pickups.

Hours of service: The legal hours, set by the Department of Transportation, a driver is allowed to drive.

Over-the-road driver or OTR driver: A long-distance truck driver running multiple states and away from home for more than one night.

Owner-operator: A truck driver who owns and operates his own truck, though it's often leased to a trucking company.

PrePass: Trucks with PrePass have a receiver/sender in the cab about the size of a small hand, which sends and receives a signal to the weigh station, allowing the truck to bypass the station when given a green light.

Q: Qualcomm, the on-board truck satellite system used to send and receive messages, including load information.

Reefer: A refrigerated trailer used to haul perishables such as fruit, vegetables, and meat. The trailer's rear doors are usually quilted aluminum with an eight-by-ten-inch viewing or air door in the bottom right corner. A refrigerated unit mounted on the front of the trailer thermostatically regulates the temperature inside the trailer.

Sleeper: The back part of a tractor's cab containing the bunks.

Split a load: To drop a loaded trailer at one of the company's drop yards. Dispatch will assign the load to another driver who will either drop it at another yard or deliver it.

Steer tires: The two front tires on a tractor.

Tandems: The two rear axles on the trailer with eight wheels that slide on rails and allow a driver to adjust the weight distribution in the trailer. The tandem weight cannot exceed thirty-four thousand pounds, and moving them forward increases the trailer overhang and weight on those axles. Moving the tandems backward reduces that weight while increasing the weight on the tractor's drive tires.

Tractor trailer: A tractor and trailer combination known as a "tractor trailer" or "eighteen-wheeler." The tractor is the truck part of the tractor trailer combination.

Weigh station: Each state has its own rules and standards, which regulate trucks operating in or passing through that state. The stations weigh trucks and check if they have the proper weight and permits for that state.

Made in the USA
Middletown, DE
18 June 2023